The New Americans
Recent Immigration and American Society

Edited by
Steven J. Gold and Rubén G. Rumbaut

A Series from LFB Scholarly

Immigrant and Native Black College Students
Social Experiences and Academic Outcomes

Audrey Alforque Thomas

LFB Scholarly Publishing LLC
El Paso 2014

Copyright © 2014 by LFB Scholarly Publishing LLC

All rights reserved.

Library of Congress Cataloging-in-Publication Data

Thomas, Audrey Alforque, 1974-
  Immigrant and native black college students : social experiences and academic outcomes / Audrey Alforque Thomas.
    pages cm. -- (The new Americans: recent immigration and American society)
  Includes bibliographical references and index.
  ISBN 978-1-59332-704-0 (hardcover : alk. paper)
  1. College students, Black--United States. 2. African American college students. 3. Immigrants--Education (Higher)--United States. 4. Children of immigrants--Education (Higher)--United States. 5. Blacks--Race identity--United States. 6. Educational surveys--United States. I. Title.
  LC2781.7.T56 2014
    378.1982996073--dc23
                                        2013034246

ISBN 978-1-59332-704-0

Printed on acid-free 250-year-life paper.

Manufactured in the United States of America.

Table of Contents

Acknowledgements

Mary Waters has challenged me to tease out sociological and theoretical issues from my findings, pushing me to elevate my work from description into the realm of analysis. Chris Avery gave excellent, continued, and detailed feedback. I am humbled by the sheer number of hours he has invested in my work. Prudence Carter has been an inspiration for me as a sociologist. She does the type of work – ambitious projects with global scope – that many in this profession can only aspire to. Orlando Patterson's work has greatly informed my own. Orlando's work speaks to all informed, engaged citizens of the world.

At Harvard, I was lucky to work with Katherine Newman, Stan Lieberson, Mary Brinton, and Mary-Jo DelVecchio Good. I benefited from the encouragement of Donna Barnes, Diane Beeson, and Benjamin Bowser at Cal State Hayward. At UC Berkeley, Erin Murphy-Graham and Irene Bloemraad gave excellent advice. Steve Chatman, Gregg Thomson, and Paula Zeszotarski were very generous with their time as I applied for access to and began to explore the University of California Undergraduate Experience Survey. I was fortunate to also discuss my research with UC Berkeley faculty Sandra Smith, Jerome Karabel, and Jabari Mahiri. I greatly benefited from the mentorship of Sandraluz Lara-Cinisomo during my internship at RAND and beyond.

I gave talks based on this research at conferences at UC Berkeley and Harvard. My work is much better for the engaged and critical dialogue with Eduardo Mosqueda, Onoso Imoagene, Van Tran, Eva Rosen, Nicole Deterding, Tomás Jimenez, and Wendy Roth, among others. My colleagues at Harvard, Katharina Pick, Victor Chen, Kirsten Hoyte, and Zoua Vang I now count among my closest friends.

I was fortunate to have funding for this research from the Association for Institutional Research / National Postsecondary Educational Consortium, American Educational Research Association, and the Harvard Graduate Society. Cynthia Verba, in the Fellowships Office, was instrumental in preparing my proposals for funding. Suzanne Washington, Lauren Dye, Genevieve Butler, Jessica Matteson and Dorothy Friendly have been my advocates and have always pulled through.

I am grateful to my informants who allowed me a glimpse into their lives, sharing their stories so willingly. I hope I have done them justice in this work.

CHAPTER 1

The Black Student in U.S. Colleges

California's Proposition 209 banned the use of racial or ethnic preferences in institutions funded by the state. I lived in Berkeley in the years after the passage of Prop 209, and I noticed the dwindling numbers of Black students. I worried about the effect this would have on the future business, political, and academic leaders in California, the nation, and the world, which is what I believe Berkeley produces. This public issue sparked a research question: How would the smaller share of Black students affect their social experience on campus? Is there an effect on non-Black students as well?

A few years later, I read with interest the revelation that many Black students at selective universities are immigrants or children of immigrants. I wondered how Black immigrants and children of Black immigrants interacted with their native Black peers within the university. Did they come together as a unified Black student group or did mutual stereotyping make them wary of each other?

The Black immigrant group is interesting when juxtaposed with native Black Americans. It is almost a natural experiment: a group of highly-educated and motivated people (as West Indian and African immigrants are) who have a socially-constructed marker that is systematically discriminated against (as Blackness is in the U.S.). Will their strong, academically-focused ethnic communities protect their children from the allure of so-called ghetto culture? Can their immigrant optimism and belief in meritocracy overcome structural and interpersonal racism?

Examining the social experiences of Black students is made richer when making comparisons across other ethnicities. Thus, one aspect of my research is the exploration of the unique Black college experience. Does the milieu of the university differ by ethnicity? Are there critical fissures between ethnic groups, making one's experiences qualitative different from another's?

PREVIOUS RESEARCH ON BLACKS IN HIGHER EDUCATION

In research on Blacks in higher education, many of the prominent researchers evaluated Black experiences and outcomes in the time of Affirmative Action (Bowen and Bok 2000, Willie 2003, Allen 1985, Zweigenhaft and Domhoff 1991). This body of work demonstrates that Black students can excel in selective universities, but there is often a price to be paid in terms of assimilation. Also, the support of other Black students is essential. It is interesting to examine Black students in this post-Affirmative Action era. It seems that mainstream society is questioning the very presence of racism (Leonhardt 2012). And several states, including California (the site of this study), have banned Affirmative Action programs. The present study examines the experiences of Black students in higher education in this new era.

In terms of the comparison of immigrant Blacks and native Blacks, theories from the immigration literature propose that there will be differences in the experiences and educational outcomes of these two groups. Ogbu (1991) offers a theoretical frame with which to understand immigrant and native Blacks. His concepts of voluntary and involuntary minorities suggest that immigrant Blacks compare their situation in the U.S. with that of their contemporaries in their home countries. By comparison, their opportunities look advantageous, and discrimination appears temporary and surmountable. With this positive dual frame of reference, immigrant Blacks will have more favorable experiences and outcomes. On the other hand, native Blacks compare their situation with that of White Americans and find their opportunities lacking. Discrimination appears as a permanent and insurmountable social fact. Their negative dual frame of reference will result in disassociation with the educational system.

In addition to Ogbu's theoretical frame, other immigration literature portends favorable outcomes for immigrants and their children. Much is made of the beneficial effects of co-ethnic and family social capital on second-generation immigrants' educational outcomes (Bankston and Zhou 1995, Portes and Zhou 1993, Portes and Rumbaut 2001). Studies specifically on the West Indian immigrant population suggest that pervasive racism in the U.S. pushes immigrant Blacks to identify with native Blacks. At the same time, the social mobility, economic success, and academic achievement of immigrant Blacks is often linked to distancing oneself from native Blacks (Waters 1999, Vickermann 1999).

The comparison of immigrant and native Black students on college campuses are just starting to emerge. These studies are finding that immigrant and native Blacks have similar rates of college matriculation (Bennett and Lutz 2009) and college grade point average (Massey, et al. 2007). Smith and Moore (2000) found that there is not much social distance between immigrant and native Blacks. These empirical pieces don't have the immigrant – native comparison as their focus, but their data allows them to present findings on this comparison. And the consensus is that there are not huge differences in these two groups in terms of college experience or outcomes. The present study contributes to this growing field, addressing the relevance of immigration theory as well as contributing to the empirical studies on the immigrant versus native Black question.

In terms of the color line, there is a lot of research and theorizing about immigrants in the U.S., the post-1965 immigrants. This is a stream of mainly non-White people – Latinos, Asians, Blacks. What will happen to these immigrants and their descendents? The last huge influx of immigrants in the early 1900s assimilated. It took a couple generations, but the descendents of those immigrants are now considered the American Mainstream. Some researchers, such as Alba and Nee (2003), suggest that assimilation to the mainstream will occur again, not for all groups, but for most. However, the situation is different than it was during the immigrant wave in the early 1900s: the economy is bifurcated and more restrictive of upward mobility, race is arguably more of a factor in the present time, and there is a continuous stream of immigrants. So, many social science researchers present alternatives to the assimilation model. The most widespread of these alternative models is segmented assimilation theory. The question that is relevant to this research is where the color line will be drawn on college campuses. The present study examines the experiences of college students by ethnic group in an attempt to ascertain the meaningful boundaries among these groups.

The specific literature on each topic is reviewed as the topic emerges in this work. At the discussion at the end of each chapter, I link the literature with the findings of this study.

BOOK OVERVIEW

In this work, I explore the Black experience in college, if it differs for native Black Americans versus Blacks with immigrant backgrounds, and how it is different from the experiences of non-Blacks, especially other racial and ethnic minority groups.

Chapter 2 is an overview of the methods and data used to answer the research questions. In order to tackle questions of disparity and discrimination, it is helpful to have a sense of the setting. In this case, the University of California system is the research site. The descriptive statistics presented in Chapter 2 address racial and ethnic, immigrant generation, gender, socioeconomic, and institutional variables within the UC system. The second half of Chapter 2 describes the interview sample collected at one UC campus.

Chapter 3 lays the groundwork for a central thesis of this work: the presence of a unique Black college experience. I argue that immigrant and native Black students share a common experience, shaped by institutional factors. I explore how campus ethnic diversity affects the social milieu of Black students, as well as taking stock of the UC system in the years following the state ban on Affirmative Action. Taking a step back, I examine differences in the social experiences of Black, Chicano/Latino, Asian, and White students. This analysis informs a discussion of the color line on college campuses.

Chapter 4 discusses the social capital of UC students, paying particular attention to Black students. Theories on college student persistence emphasize the importance of social capital to college graduation. The statistical analysis presents a puzzle in that Black students belong to dense and varied social networks on campus, yet have a low graduation rate. I argue that social capital is a necessary factor for Black student retention but not a sufficient one for Black student graduation.

Chapters 4 and 5 show the unity of the Black student community, regardless of family immigration history. The Black student community provides empathy as well as academic support to its members. I argue that the small number of Black students on campus coupled with a hostile racial environment necessitate a cohesive and, to some degree, insular Black student community. This community is so influential to Black students that it defines their social integration into the campus.

Chapter 5 examines perceptions of discrimination across ethnicities and the effects of discrimination on educational outcomes. I offer additional support for the continued existence of a Black – non-Black color line. I also continue the argument that immigrant and native Black students have similar experiences on campus. The main finding of this chapter is the omnipresent threat of negative stereotypes for Blacks in the academic arena.

In Chapter 6, I evaluate the effects of socioeconomic, cultural, and intellectual integration factors on graduation from college. The link between immigrant and native Black students' similarities in experiences and similarities in outcomes is made explicit in Chapter 6. In addition, I argue that the institution of the university discourages the intellectual integration of Black students, negatively affecting their likelihood of graduating.

Chapter 7 concludes by bringing together the common themes running through the substantive chapters. Namely, there is a Black student experience that is common to native Black Americans, and 1.5- and second-generation Black immigrants. Influenced by their underrepresentation on campus, persistent interpersonal racism, and insensitive institutional policies, Black students rely upon the Black student community for psychological, social, and academic support. The other theme that emerges from this research is a Black student experience that is unique to Black students. On myriad measures of social experience, Black students are set apart from White and Asian students, and even different from Chicano/Latino students. I offer evidence-based implications for university policy. The policy implications focus on the ways the institution can better support and nurture Black students.

I also reflect on the intractability of the Black – non-Black color line. The university, especially the public university, is a promising arena in which to foster social change. The university has the power to bring young people of different ethnicities together as peers. Integration, especially in this sensitive period of identity formation in college, breeds tolerance. Fostering interethnic interactions among students in a supportive environment will revitalize what Orlando Patterson has called ecumenical America, a nation of patriots that value each citizen's rich cultural background.

CHAPTER 2

Black Students in the University of California System

The motivating questions for this research project were: How do Black students experience college? Does this experience vary based on immigrant generation? Is it different than the experience of students of other ethnicities? What factors affect the academic performance of Black college students? I used mixed methods to address the questions. The quantitative dataset includes University of California (UC) students enrolled during Spring term 2004 who chose to complete the University of California Undergraduate Experience Survey (UCUES). The qualitative data consists of 39 interviews with Black undergraduate students at one UC campus during the academic year 2007-08.

UNIVERSITY OF CALIFORNIA UNDERGRADUATE EXPERIENCE SURVEY

The University of California Undergraduate Experience Survey (UCUES) 2004 compiles data from undergraduates at UC campuses during the Spring term 2004. Data comes from eight of the ten UC campuses since UC San Francisco does not have undergraduate students and the UC Merced campus opened in 2005. The eight campuses in the dataset are: Berkeley, Davis, Irvine, Los Angeles, Riverside, Santa Barbara, Santa Cruz, and San Diego.

Of the 153,672 undergraduates enrolled at UC campuses during the 2004 Spring term, 51,819 (33.7%) responded to the survey. Data from students' UC applications were added to give information on ethnicity, high school grade point average, and SAT I score. UC grade point average in Spring 2004 and academic status for Spring term 2007 were

7

supplied by the Office of the Registrar. The UCUES contains variables that are difficult to find in other surveys of college students and that were necessary for this project. In particular, variables on birth country of students, their parents, and their grandparents enabled me to assign each student to an immigrant generation. Thus, it was possible to compare the experiences and academic outcomes of immigrant Black and native Black UC students.

Ethnicity
The ethnicity data are based on the University of California application. Prospective students complete one UC application, which is sent to the campuses the prospective student selects. The data is comparable across the campuses because each respondent was asked the same question about their ethnicity. Pan-ethnic categories, such as "Asian" and "Chicano/Latino" are problematic because of the great variation among the ethnicities conflated within them. Unfortunately, finer distinctions are not possible in this study.

Figure 2.1 represents UC undergraduates enrolled during spring 2004. Asian and White students make up the majority of the University of California undergraduate population. Chicano/Latinos are the next largest ethnic category. Black is the smallest ethnic category. The remaining students chose "Other" or "Decline to State" for their ethnicity. There is a sizeable group of respondents who refuse to answer and those who choose "Other" without the opportunity to specify what that means to them.

Ethnic group representation in the UC system
Black students are a small percentage of the University of California campuses, a much smaller proportion than in the general California population (Figure 2.2). Of college-age people in California[1], 6.6% are Black (State of California, Department of Finance, 2009); however, only 3.1% of UC students are Black. Other races have a disproportionate absence or presence in the UC system as well. Most

---

[1] College-aged are people from the ages of 18 to 25. Data from the state of California is from 2000 because it is the latest year for which there is U.S. Census data that allows the separation of the Black population into immigrant and native.

notably, Hispanics (as they are called by the State of California) make up 40.7% of the college-aged population but Chicano/Latinos (the terms used by the University of California) are a scant 13.7% of UC students. The overrepresented group is Asians[2]: they comprise 12.6% of the college-aged population in the state, but 37.9% of the UC population.

Figure 2.1: Ethnicity of University of California students (n = 152,714)

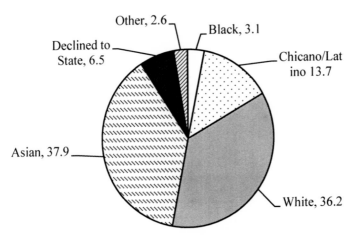

Missing = 958

---

[2] The state of California has separate categories for "Asian" and "Pacific Islander." I conflate these categories to make them comparable to the University of California category "Asian" which includes Asians and Pacific Islanders.

Figure 2.2: Ethnicity of University of California students and college-age Californians

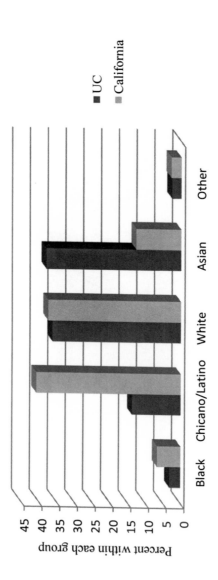

UC students, n = 152,714; State of California, n = 3,765,622

The UC percentages do not add up to 100 percent because the category Refused (6.5%) is omitted. This was necessary since there is no comparable category for the state of California data. The state of California data does not add up to 100 percent because of rounding.

State of California, Department of Finance (2009)

Immigrant generation

Theoretically and empirically, it is important to differentiate immigrant generations. In the U.S. immigration literature, an immigrant or first-generation immigrant is commonly defined as a person who comes to the U.S. as an adult, usually older than 12 years old. Those who immigrate to the U.S. as children are called 1.5-generation immigrants. A second-generation immigrant is someone born in the U.S. to at least one foreign-born parent; some researchers require that the mother be the immigrant.

Due to the small number of Black students and particularly the low number of Black students from immigrant families, it was necessary to combine immigrants, 1.5-generation immigrants, and second-generation immigrants into one category to compare with native Blacks. This strategy is acceptable because all informants belong to the same age cohort[3], so their experiences in the U.S. are similar to the extent that they are temporally bound. Extant empirical work shows that, for many immigrant groups, immigrants and second-generation immigrants are more similar to each other than to a comparable native group (Hagy and Staniec 2002, Glick and White 2004, Rong and Brown 2001). Also, other studies of the college experience have collapsed the second-generation, 1.5-generation, and immigrants into one immigrant category (Massey, Mooney, Torres, and Charles 2007).

In Figure 2.3, I separate students into immigrant and native categories within each ethnicity. Asian and Chicano/Latino students are overwhelmingly immigrant or second-generation immigrant. Blacks and Whites are mostly native. In Chapter 3, I compare the proportions of immigrant and native Blacks in the UC system to the proportions of immigrant and native Blacks in California.

Gender

Within the Black community, there is a striking difference in the college-going rates by gender. Many more Black women than men attend postsecondary institutions. Females make up 64% of the Blacks undergraduates across the U.S. (NCES 2005) and 63% of Black UC

---

[3] Almost all undergraduates are less than 25 years old. In Fall 2001, only 4% of students admitted to UC's were older than 25 (Galligani 2003) and most students (87%) graduate within six years (The Education Trust 2007).

students. The Black gender gap is larger than for any other racial category, but it is important to note that each group has its own gender gap, both at U.S. colleges in general and in the UC system (Table 2.1).

Figure 2.3: Immigrant generation by ethnicity, n = 38,916

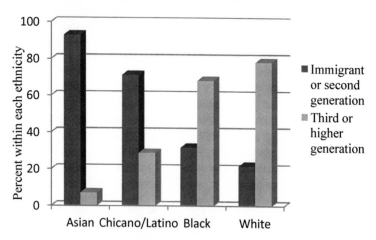

Explanations for the Black gender gap in high education center mainly around economic opportunities. The knowledge that economic mobility after college is blocked may discourage academic achievement in minority men (Ogbu 1987). Similarly, poor academic performance or dropping out of school can be viewed as a critique of the inequalities present in the educational system and labor market (McDaniel, DiPrete, Buchmann, Shwed 2011, Fine and Rosenberg 1983, Carter 2005, Taylor, Casten, Flickinger, and Roberts 1994). However, other researchers have found that Black men's college attendance is not affected by economic returns to education. Kane (1994), using data from the U.S. Census Current Population Survey, found that the Black male college enrollment rate was not affected by post-college employment rates. In an evaluation of the hypothesis that young men and women act as econometricians when making post-high school plans, Beattie (2002), using High School and Beyond data, came to the same conclusion: young Black men's post-secondary enrollment was unaffected by returns to schooling.

The Black gender gap in higher education exists but is not as pronounced among immigrant Blacks. Whereas 25% of native Black students are male, the figure is 32% for immigrant Black students. Similarly, Massey et al (2007) discovered that the gender gap in college matriculation holds for both native Blacks and immigrant Blacks. In terms of educational attainment once in college, there is some difference by gender. Although they do not discuss the results, Massey and colleagues found that the effect of being female is strong and positive for native Blacks' grade point average, but not significant for immigrant Blacks' college grades. The researchers are unable to comment on why these factors differentially affect native and immigrant Blacks. Since it is an important variable, a control for gender is included in all UCUES regression analyses throughout this work.

Table 2.1: Representation of female students, by ethnicity

	U.S. colleges	UC system
Black	64%	63%
White	56%	53%
Asian	54%	54%
Hispanic	59%	60%

National Center for Education Statistics (2005)
UC students, n = 138,832

Socioeconomic status
It is typical for college students to have higher family social capital than their non-college-going peers. That is, the parents of college students are more likely to have college and advanced degrees and belong to higher income brackets (Bailey and Dynarski 2011, Espenshade and Radford 2009, Deil-Amen and Turley 2007). The findings from UC students follow this pattern.

UC students differ from the general population of California and the U.S. The educational attainment of UC parents is higher than state and national distributions (Figure 2.4). The modal category of educational attainment for U.S. adults is a high school diploma and for California adults is some college or an associate's degree. However, the most common level of education for mothers of UC students is a college degree and for fathers, an advanced degree. Not surprisingly, the median household income of UC parents ($64,000) is also greater than in the general population ($44,700) (U.S. Census 2004a). Even in a state with a high average household income at $51,200 (U.S. Census 2004b), UC families are another notch above.

Families of UC students may differ greatly from the California and U.S. population in general, but there are also disparities within UC students. White students are likely to come from middle- and high-income families (household income greater than $50,000); the modal household income for Black and Chicano/Latino students is less than $50,000 (Figure 2.5). The data on levels of father's education is presented in Figure 2.6. The pattern is similar for mother's education. Glancing at the mode for each ethnicity is telling: an advanced degree is the most common educational level for parents of White UC students, while less than high school is the mode for Chicano/Latino UC students. Some college is the most common educational level for parents of Black UC students. The parents of Asian students are likely to have a bachelor's degree, but they are also highly represented among those with less than a high school diploma. This suggests great heterogeneity in the academic attainment of Asian UC students' parents.

To illustrate, in a small way, the difference that socioeconomic status can have on a college student's experience, I present the results from a UCUES question: "How often did you need and use the Financial Aid Office?" (Figure 2.7). Black student respondents chose the answer, "Used it often" much more frequently than students of other ethnicities (significant at the 0.001 level).

Socioeconomic factors vary greatly by ethnicity and are important contributors to academic performance and attainment, so regression models predicting educational outcomes include parents' education and household income. In Chapter 6, I examine differences in parental education and income between immigrant and native Black students.

Institutional comparisons

To follow the rules regarding the use of the UCUES dataset, I did not name the campuses when conducting institutional analyses. Instead, I created categories of campuses based on conceptually important factors. For some analyses, the campuses are grouped by the proportion of Black students on campus or the proportion of underrepresented minorities. In other analyses, the selectivity of the campus was critical.

Figure 2.4: Educational attainment of UC parents, U.S. adults, and California adults

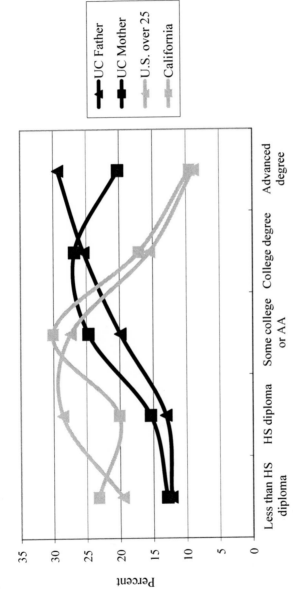

(Bauman and Graf 2003)

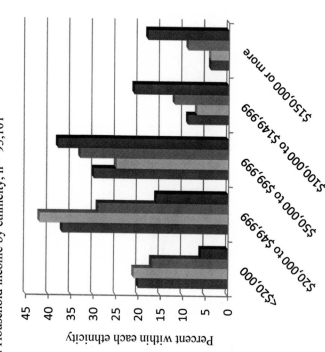

Figure 2.5: Household income by ethnicity, n = 93,101

Figure 2.6: Father's education by ethnicity, n = 110,000

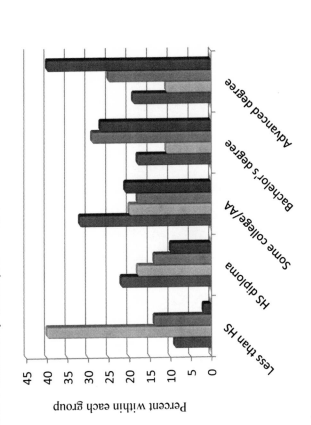

Percent within each group

Less than HS
HS diploma
Some college/AA
Bachelor's degree
Advanced degree

■ Black
■ Latino
■ Asian
■ White

Figure 2.7: Need and use the Financial Aid Office, by ethnicity (n = 37,602)

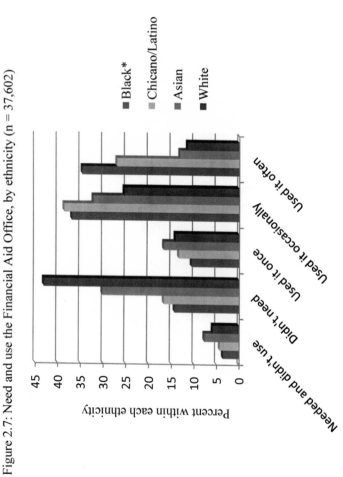

*Chi-square significant at the 0.001 level

To create the categories based on ethnic diversity, I looked at the proportions of each ethnicity (Figure 2.8). Berkeley and Los Angeles have similar ethnic breakdowns: a majority Asian campus with a significant percentage of White students. San Diego has similar proportions of Asians and Whites to the flagship campuses, but with less than half the representation of Black students than Berkeley and Los Angeles. Santa Barbara and Santa Cruz stand out because of their low percentages of Asians relative to other campuses. By far, the majority of their students are White. They have a sizeable percentage of Chicano/Latinos, but their percentage of Blacks is low. Irvine is marked by its high percentage of Asian students. Riverside is the most ethnically diverse campus. It has the highest percentage of Black students and Chicano/Latino students. It is a majority Asian campus and has the lowest percentage of White students.

To understand how campus selectivity might operate, I divided the eight UC campuses into categories based on the high school academic performance of their students (Figure 2.9). The criteria were average high school GPA and SAT I scores of the incoming freshmen class in 2004. Three categories emerged based on selectivity: Flagship campuses, Competitive campuses, and Less Competitive campuses. The Flagship campuses of the UC system are among the most selective colleges in the nation. The competitiveness of admission to these schools is comparable to New York University and University of Michigan, Ann Arbor. The Competitive campuses' selectively of admissions is comparable to University of Massachusetts, Amherst and University of Washington, Seattle. Less Competitive campuses are the least selective of the eight colleges in this study, with the lowest average SAT I scores and high school grade point averages for incoming freshmen. Comparable colleges are State University of New York, Albany and Ohio University.

Educational outcomes
Most students who were enrolled in the Spring term 2004 had graduated (87.2%) by the Spring term 2007. A very small percentage (0.8%) was still enrolled. For the purposes of this study, I combined graduated and continuing students, and contrasted them with those who had withdrawn (12.0%). Persistence in college varies by campus selectivity.

Figure 2.8: Ethnicity of University of California students by campus (n = 152,714)

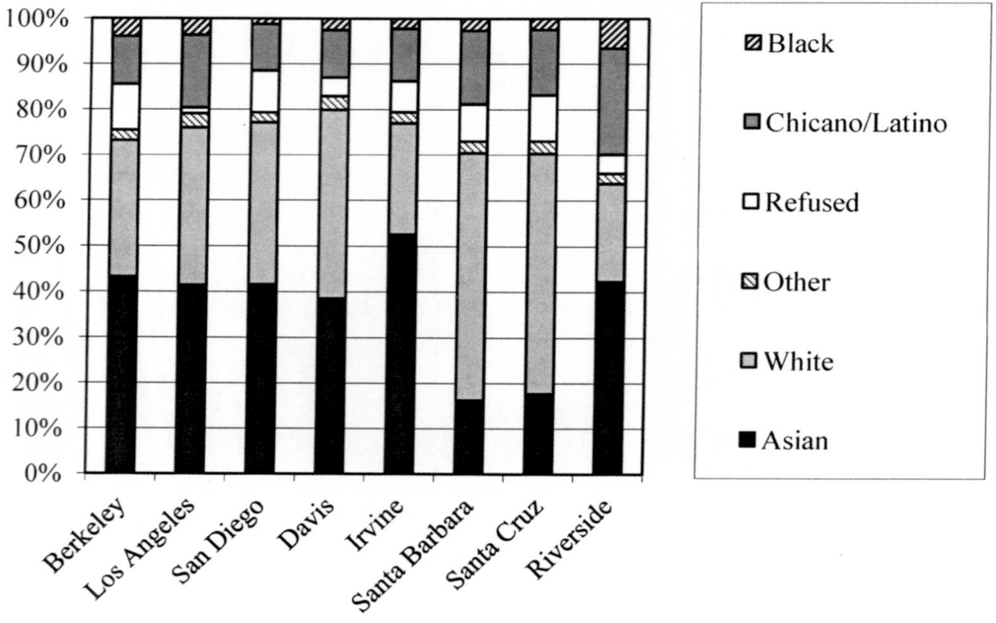

Figure 2.9: Academic selectivity of University of California campuses

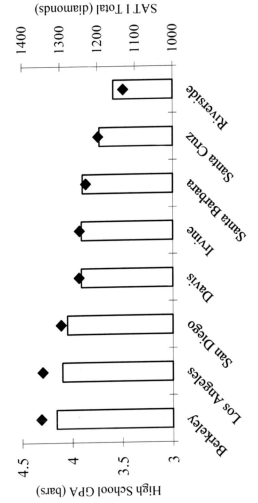

Bars represent high school grade point average (left axis) and diamonds represent SAT I total (right axis). California Freshman Admit Profile Fall 2004. Source: University of California Office of the President, Student Affairs, Office of Undergraduate Admissions, "UCAP March-end, 2004."

As expected based on the literature, students at more selective campuses are more likely to graduate (Gansemer-Topf 2006, Baker and Velez 1996, Tinto 1993). In the present study, the graduation rate at flagship campuses was 92%, compared to 88% at competitive and 81% at less competitive campuses. Also in line with current literature, Black and Chicano/Latino students have lower graduation rates than White and Asian students (Murtaugh, Burns, Schuster 1999, Baker and Velez 1996). Within the UC system, the graduation rates of Asian and Whites are both 89%. That figure is 83% for Chicano/Latinos and 79% for Blacks.

QUALITATIVE DATA

I spent 20 months at one UC campus and interviewed 39 Black students there to add rich qualitative data to the research project. I spent a great deal of time in a busy student study center, observed students on the main plaza of the campus, and attended cultural events put on by student groups.

Recruitment

I recruited interviewees through Black student groups, then through snowball sampling. In the initial analysis of the interviews, the importance of the Black community on campus emerged. In order to reach Black students who were not part of Black student groups, I solicited interviewees before classes (with the permission of the instructors) and approached Black students on campus.

Interview protocol

I began each interview with a questionnaire containing closed-ended questions (see Appendix) about demographic information, family immigration history, socioeconomic status, and educational aspirations and expectations. I read the questionnaires to the respondents and wrote down their answers. The in-depth interviews were recorded using a digital voice recorder. The questions covered general college experience, ethnic identity and networks, experiences of discrimination on campus, evaluation of instructors' and classmates' attitudes toward the respondent, gender differences within the respondent's family, and perceived differences between native and immigrant Blacks (see Appendix for a list of in-depth questions).

One year after each interview, I invited the respondent to complete an online follow-up survey (see Appendix). They were asked their enrollment status at the UC they were attending at the time of the original interview, if they had experienced discrimination on campus since the interview, and their UC grade point average.

Analysis

I used grounded theory methodology to analyze the interviews and to direct data collection. The transcripts were open coded line-by-line to allow actions and processes to emerge from the data. Using grounded theory methodology privileges the voices of the interviewees, allowing them to determine the course of the analysis (Glaser and Strauss 1967). I did, however, use themes from the literature and statistical analysis to inform the coding procedure. These sensitizing concepts were starting points for analysis rather than rigid categories to force data into (Charmaz 2000). After categories emerged from the initial coding, I conducted a second, more directed round of coding. During both the open and focused coding, I wrote memos which elaborated on the categories, examined conditions of the categories, and predicted consequences. From these memos, larger themes and connections became apparent. These became the substantive chapters of this work.

Demographic information

At the time of the interview, each respondent was an undergraduate at one UC campus. The average age of the respondents was 19.6 years. They ranged in age from 18 to 25 years old. Despite strongly recruiting Black males for the study, my sample reflects the larger gender imbalance of the Black UC community (Table 2.1). I sought to have an even number of male and female respondents; however, of the 39 respondents, only 11 are male.

The country of birth for the respondents' parents is presented in Table 2.2. Nineteen of the respondents had U.S.-born parents. These are the native Black respondents. The remaining 20 had at least one parent born in an African country. I call these respondents immigrant Blacks.

All of the native Black respondents and 18 of the 20 immigrant Black respondents identified their race as "Black or African American." There was much more variation in the way interviewees described their ethnicity, which was an open-ended question. In Chapter 3, I discuss the racial and ethnic categories that the respondents chose on the questionnaire, as well as their struggles with those categories.

Most of the native Black students identified as "Black," but this was true of only one immigrant Black student. The immigrant Black students were a mix between those who identified only with their ethnicity, for example "Nigerian," and those who chose a hyphenated identity, such as "Nigerian American." A detailed discussion of these ethnic identifiers is presented in Chapter 3.

Table 2.2: Birthplace of parents and respondents

Country of birth	Number
of both parents – U.S.	19
of at least one parent – Nigeria	12
of at least one parent – Ethiopia	5
of at least one parent – Eritrea	2
of at least one parent – Sudan	1

The questionnaire had socioeconomic questions about parental and sibling education, and parents' income and work. I also asked how the interviewee was paying for tuition and living expenses. Levels of parental education were in line with empirical research (Dodoo 1997, Djamba 1999, Bennett and Lutz 2009) and the larger UCUES dataset (Figure 2.6). That is, immigrant Black fathers were much more likely to have a college or graduate degree (Figure 2.10). The educational advantage held for mothers, but to a lesser extent. There was not much difference by immigrant generation in household income or home ownership for the interview respondents. The modal annual household income was between $40,000 and $79,999. Respondents were evenly split in terms of parental home ownership (Rent, n = 18; Own, n = 21).

There was no difference by immigrant generation in terms of how respondents were paying for tuition or living expenses, which makes sense given the similarities in family incomes for immigrant and native Blacks. Most respondents have scholarships for tuition (n = 30) and living expenses (n = 23). Many use multiple sources to cover living expenses, including parents' out-of-pocket spending and respondents working.

Figure 2.10: Educational attainment of respondents' fathers, by immigrant generation (n = 39)

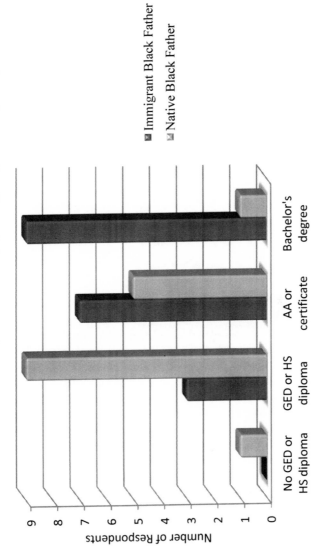

Educational Outcomes

I also asked about the interviewee's educational aspirations and expectations. Thirty-eight of the 39 respondents aspired to a graduate degree, and 35 believed they would attain this aspiration. When asked about finishing college, 37 of the 39 interview respondents unequivocally said they would. This is not surprising, given the high ambitions of many young people (Schneider and Stevenson 1999). In particular, Black students may decouple their ambitions from their academic achievements. Knowing in the abstract that school is the path to upward mobility does not automatically translate into academic success (Ainsworth-Darnell and Downey 1998, Carter 2005). Based on a study of Black students at predominantly White public universities, Allen (1985:146) commented, "To a surprising extent, these students seem to set their aspirations outside consideration of their demonstrated academic abilities."

Respondents completed an online survey one year after the interview. Thirty-seven of the 39 interviewees responded (95% response rate). Of the 37, 36 were still enrolled as full time students at the same campus or had graduated. One had left the UC school and was enrolled at a community college.

CONCLUSION

Throughout the chapters, I also use UCUES data to examine differences in the college experiences of immigrant versus native Blacks. Using longitudinal academic status data, I examined the relationships between crucial experiential factors and academic outcomes.

The qualitative data provides descriptions of the experiences of Black college students. For example, a finding from UCUES is that Black students are less likely than White students to feel a sense of belonging on campus. The interviewees recounted the ways they felt left out or misunderstood. In this way, the interview data creates a rich backdrop for the statistical analysis. The synthesis of the UCUES statistical data and qualitative interview material create a nuanced portrait of Black college student experiences within the UC system and at one campus in particular.

CHAPTER 3

The Black College Experience

What are the meaningful boundaries among ethnic groups on college campuses? I examine this question quantitatively and determine how the *color line* is drawn on UC campuses. Between which groups do socially meaningful boundaries exist? Secondly, I examine how ethnic diversity operates across campuses with different levels of diversity. How does the ethnic makeup of a college affect the social experiences and educational outcomes of its students? Lastly, I use interview data to explore how immigrant and native Black students identify themselves at one campus. Are there two separate Black groups, divided by family immigration history, or is there a unified Black community?

RELEVANT LITERATURE

The color line on campus
By examining ethnicity in the arena of higher education, the present study contributes to the current question of the color line in the United States. With increasing numbers of Latinos, Blacks, and Asians, from both immigration and the birth of second-generation immigrants, and increasing numbers of multiracial people, social scientists are re-drawing the traditional Black-White color line in the United States (Alba and Nee 2003). It is unclear what the consequential distinction(s) will be: White and non-White; Black and non-Black; White, honorary white, and black collective; or some other permutation. Recent studies suggest that Latinos and Asians are becoming politically and socially closer to, and perhaps merging with, White Americans (Sears and Savalei 2006, Sears, Fu, Henry, and Bui 2007) and the critical color line will emerge between Blacks and non-

Blacks (Lee and Bean 2007, Sears, Fu, Henry, and Bui 2007). Given the large representation of Asians in the UC system and their image, whether based on fact or fiction, as "model minority" and "honorary Whites" (Zhou 2004, Tuan 1998, Lee 1996), it is possible that the significant distinctions are White, honorary White, and Black collective (comprised of Black and Chicano/Latino students).

Two recent studies set in selective universities have examined the issue of interracial student interaction (Espenshade and Radford 2009, Massey, et al. 2003). The studies concur that the greatest interracial social *closeness* is between Hispanics and Whites, then between Asians and Whites. Espenshade and Radford (2009) went on to show that the greatest social distance was between non-Blacks and Blacks.

The effects of campus diversity
There is an ongoing public debate about the importance of ethnic diversity at universities. Orlando Patterson (1997) persuasively argues that diversity on college campuses is necessary for the cross-pollination of ethnic communities, in order to encourage a united, yet pluralistic U.S. society. Interethnic interaction has been linked to educational and social benefits. Studies have shown increases in the civic engagement and democratic beliefs of students who have interethnic interactions (Gurin, et al. 2002, Hurtado 2005). Interactions with students of other ethnicities are also positively related to educational measures such as openness to different viewpoints and self-assessed academic skills (Espenshade and Radford 2009, Gurin, et al. 2002, Hurtado 2005). Scholarly work suggests that increasing the ethnic diversity on a campus will result in increased interethnic interaction. In a critical review of this literature, Justin Pidot (2006:783) concludes, "many would anticipate that increasing the number of students of color at a university would increase the amount of cross-racial interaction. The data available suggest that this is at least modestly so." Certainly students who learn in ethnically diverse environments are able to live and work in ethnically diverse environments (Bowen and Bok 2000).

While the benefits of interethnic interaction have been empirically shown, there is still some uncertainty about how university administrators can encourage interethnic interaction. The assumption is that increasing diversity will increase interethnic interaction, but this cannot be taken for granted.

Black identity on campus
Given that college is a time of detachment from the natal family and immersion in a culture that encourages self-exploration, how do Black students identify their ethnicity? Based on the existing literature, we should expect that native and immigrant Black students will espouse identifiers that separate the two groups. According to John Ogbu's (1991) theory on voluntary immigrants and involuntary minorities, native Blacks are expected to identify themselves in opposition to Whites. In the context of the college campus, this may mean choosing one strong identifier, such as "Black" or "African American." On the other hand, immigrant Blacks would be expected to choose a nationalistic identity and make their identifier distinct from native Blacks.

Empirical research on West Indian immigrants and their children shows this desire to create an identity separate from native Blacks (Vickerman 1999, Kasinitz, et al. 2008). From a study including second-generation West Indian teenagers, Mary Waters (1999:324) concluded, "The more socially mobile the individual, the more he or she clings to ethnic identity as a hedge against racial identity." We should expect that the immigrant Black students, who are socially mobile since they attend a selective university, to socially distance themselves from native Black students. In a study of first- and second-generation West Indians in college, Kay Deaux (2006) found that these immigrant Blacks rate their own group more favorably than they rate African Americans (Deaux 2006). Massey and colleagues (2006) disaggregated Black students at selective colleges by native versus immigrant, and discovered that immigrant Blacks were more likely than native Blacks to choose "Other" as their ethnicity. These studies suggest that native and immigrant Black college students will define themselves differently, and that immigrant Blacks will distinguish themselves from native Blacks. However, Waters (1999) also discussed the ways that West Indian immigrants and their children, especially those who are poor or working class, are constantly assaulted with the realities of racial discrimination in the U.S. She found that persistent racism can affect the way young people identify themselves.

FINDINGS FROM THE QUANTITATIVE DATA

Diversity of UC students

The ethnic diversity of the UC system does not reflect California's population. As reviewed in Chapter 2, Blacks and Chicano/Latinos are underrepresented on UC campuses (Figure 2.2). While almost 7% of college-age Californians are Black, only 3% of UC students are Black. Over 40% of Californians aged 18-25 are Hispanic while less than 15% of UC students identify as Chicano/Latino. The overrepresented ethnic group is Asian. Their figures are almost the exact converse of Chicano/Latino's: about 13% of the college-aged population in California is Asian, but almost 40% of the UC population is Asian. The ethnic makeup of individual campuses varies greatly (Figure 2.8), so it is possible to explore how a university's ethnic diversity affects students' social outcomes.

The color line on campus

Using social experience questions from UCUES, I explore how students of different ethnicities view their place on campus. Examining how ethnic groups are arrayed according to these social experience variables gives insight into the color line on campus. I gauge social experience using responses to two statements: "I feel I belong at this campus" and "Students are respected here regardless of their race or ethnicity." For each statement, respondents were given six choices ranging from "Strongly Disagree" (1) to "Strongly Agree" (6).

For this study, the color line is defined by the way that groups of students perceive their place on campus. If there are systematic differences by ethnicity, then members of certain groups lack a sense of belonging or feel less respected on campus. Thus, the color line is used to express how a student's place on the spectrum of college social experiences is affected by her ethnicity.

The variable about respect is a measure of perceived discrimination on campus. Disrespect for others based on their race is racial discrimination. If a respondent feels that students are respected on campus regardless of race, then they do not believe that racial discrimination is a problem. The data is such that pan-ethnic categories cannot be parsed. The ethnic categories used for comparison are: Asian, Black, Chicano/Latino, and White. Thus, these findings can be used as a starting point for further research that is able to isolate finer ethnic categories.

On the statement, "Students are respected here regardless of their race or ethnicity," Chicano/Latino, Asian, and White student responses peaked at "Agree" (Figure 3.1). Most White students (61%) agree or strongly agree that students are respected at their schools regardless of race. This figure is high for Asian students as well at 52%. Chicano/Latino students' answers were more spread out among the six choices, but Black students' responses had an altogether different pattern. This concurs with research that suggests that Latinos perceive less ethnic injustice than African Americans (Schmader, Major, and Gramzow 2001). Black student responses were highest at "Somewhat Agree" (Figure 3.1). Only 25% of Black students agree or strongly agree that students are respected on campus regardless of race. Also, a greater proportion of Black students strongly disagreed or disagreed with the statement, as compared with students of other ethnicities. Other studies have found that Black students have the highest degree of dissatisfaction with the social/racial environment in college (Hurtado 1992, Harper and Hurtado 2007). The results show the difference in experiences of discrimination by ethnicity and a strong Black/non-Black division.

The variable about belonging speaks to students' intellectual integration into the university. Tinto (1993) describes intellectual integration as students perceiving that their values are aligned with the university's values. If there are significant differences in feelings of belonging by ethnicity, this suggests that some groups of students feel that their concerns and needs are not addressed by the university. These students are made to feel that they do not belong on campus. Black students are different from other ethnic groups in terms of feeling a sense of belonging at UC campuses (Figure 3.2). White, Asian, and Chicano/Latino student responses peak at "Agree," while the Black student responses peak at "Somewhat Agree." Over 10% of Black students, compared with about 5% for each of the other groups, strongly disagree with the statement "I feel that I belong at this campus." The effects of intellectual integration on educational outcomes are modeled and discussed in detail in Chapter 6. In this chapter, I focus on the predictors of intellectual integration.

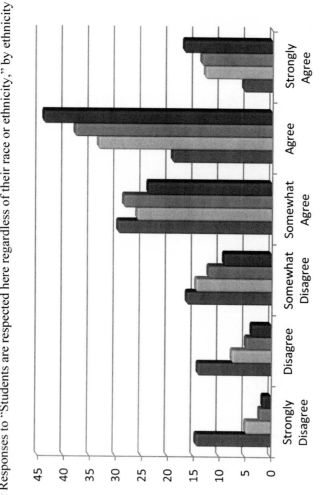

Figure 3.1: Responses to "Students are respected here regardless of their race or ethnicity," by ethnicity (n = 41,773)

Figure 3.2: Responses to "I feel I belong at this campus," by ethnicity (n = 37,818)

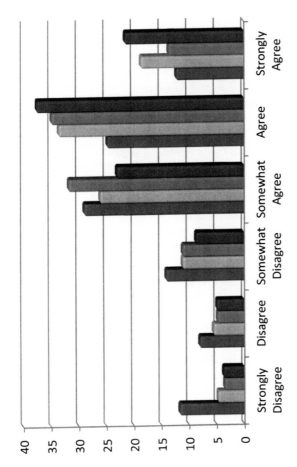

Based on these two indicators, feeling respected and sense of belonging, it is clear that Black UC students, versus students of other ethnicities, have a qualitatively different college experience. Black students are less likely to feel respected and less likely to feel they belong on campus. In comparison, Asian, Chicano/Latino, and White students are similar to each other on these measures. These findings suggest that the color line is between Black and non-Black students.

Effects of campus diversity

In order to test the effect of diversity on student experience, I use the ethnic makeup of the campus to predict social experience variables. I vary the statistical models on three dimensions: measure of diversity, social experience variable, and population.

In terms of measures of diversity, I use (1) the percent of Black or underrepresented minority (Black and Chicano/Latino) students at the campus, or (2) categories of campuses based on proportion of Black or underrepresented minority students. This results in four different explanatory variables: (a) percent Black at the campus, (b) percent underrepresented minority students at the campus, (c) categories representing campuses with the lowest, low, high, and highest proportions of Black students, and (d) categories representing campuses with the lowest, low, high, and highest proportions of underrepresented minority students. There is a distinction between these two types of measures. In the first variable, there is an assumption of a linear relationship between the percent of the student body that is Black and the outcome variable. The second allows a more complex relationship between the ethnic composition of a group of campuses and the outcome variable. By grouping campuses, I can determine the point at which minority representation matters. That is, if an outcome variable shows a significant difference between campuses with the *lowest* percents of Black students versus campuses with *low* percents of Black students, then a critical mass of Black students affects that outcome variable. Such a finding would suggest the point at which the percent of Black students reaches critical mass for the outcome variable.

Student social experience is measured in several ways: feelings of belongingness on campus, feeling respected on campus, and in-depth conversations with students of a different ethnicity. I discussed the first two variables in detail in the preceding section. The last variable, about interethnic interaction, comes from this closed question in UCUES: "How often have you had in-depth conversations with students of a different race/ethnicity?" I discuss this variable in detail in Chapter 4. Note that the relative numbers of co-ethnics will affect the probability of a student having a conversation with a student of a different ethnicity. The salient finding in this context is that Black students engaged in interethnic conversations more frequently than did students of other ethnicities. In this chapter, I examine the relationship between campus ethnic diversity and interethnic interactions.

The last dimension of variation in the models is population. For many of these statistical models, selecting only Black respondents is sensible. For example, when testing the effect of the percent of Black students at a campus on whether students feel a sense of belonging, it is logical to select for only Black students. There is no theoretical reason to test this relationship on other ethnic groups. However, when testing the effect of the percent of Black students at a campus on the frequency of interethnic conversations, I look at each ethnic group. An increasing proportion of Black students probably increases the likelihood that a student of another ethnicity will have a conversation with a Black student. In addition, when measuring diversity in terms of underrepresented minorities, I examine the outcome variables for Chicano/Latino students.

For each statistical model, I present the full model with all explanatory variables. Each model controls for: family immigration status (if the respondent is an immigrant or second-generation immigrant), parental income, mother's education, father's education, high school grade point average, SAT score or ACT equivalent, and UC grade point average. The presentation of the regression models in this chapter differ from conventional presentation. Usually additional variables are added and nested models are given successive numerical labels. Since every model presented in this chapter has all the explanatory variables, I label the models using letters rather than numbers.

"Students are respected here regardless of their race or ethnicity"
I found evidence that having a critical mass of Black students on campus is related to Black students feeling respected at that campus. In

Table 3.1, Model A, diversity is measured in terms of the percent of Black students on campus. The representation of Black students on campus is directly and significantly related to Black students feeling respected. In Table 3.1, Model B, campuses are placed in categories based on the percent of Black students on campus. The odds of a Black student feeling respected at a campus with the highest percent Black is more than 8 times greater than for a Black student at a campus with the lowest percent Black. The difference among the campuses with the lowest, low, and high levels of diversity are not significant.[4] The only significant difference in terms of campus is between the campuses with the highest levels of diversity versus all the other campuses. While other institutional factors may affect Black students' feeling respected, the results support the idea that a critical mass of Black students is needed for Black students to feel respected on campus. The critical mass is above the UC average of Black student representation.

Results are similar for Black students when diversity is measured in terms of underrepresented minorities on campus. In Table 3.1, Model C, diversity is measured in terms of the percent of underrepresented minorities on campus. The percent of underrepresented minorities on campus is directly and significantly related to Black students feeling respected. In Table 3.1, Model D, the campus categories are based on the percent of underrepresented minorities. There is a significant difference between campuses with the highest levels of diversity versus all other campuses. The odds of a Black student feeling respected at a campus with the highest level of diversity is 4.7 times greater than for a Black student at a campus with the lowest level of diversity. These results suggest that a critical mass of underrepresented minorities is important to Black students feeling respected on campus.

I now turn to a different population of students to examine the effect of diversity on feeling respected on campus. Regression models based on Chicano and Latino students are presented in Table 3.2. The results are similar to those already presented for Black students. In

---

[4] A model using Low Percent Black student campuses as the reference category, showed no difference between Low Percent Black student campuses and High Percent Black student campuses. This model is not shown.

Table 3.2, Model A, diversity is measured in terms of the percent of underrepresented minorities on campus. This variable is significantly related to Chicano/Latino students feeling respected on campus. In Table 3.2, Model B, the campus categories are based on the percent of underrepresented minorities. There is a significant difference between campuses with the highest level of diversity versus all other campuses. However, the magnitude of the effect is less for Chicano/Latino students versus Black students. Compared with Chicano/Latino students at campuses with the least amount of diversity, those at campuses with the highest amount of diversity are only 2 times more likely to feel respected.

Unlike the model for Black students, there is also a significant difference among campuses with a high percentage of underrepresented minorities versus campuses with the lowest representation. The results here are unexpected. Chicano/Latino students at campuses with a high level of diversity are *less* likely to feel respected when compared to Chicano/Latino students at campuses with the lowest level of diversity. This finding is counterintuitive, and points to the importance of using categories of campuses as explanatory variables rather than using the simple percent of underrepresented minorities on campus. I found that while the percent of underrepresented minorities on campus is positively and significantly related to Chicano/Latino students feeling respected, there are other institutional factors at play. That is, unmeasured institutional characteristics may be affecting whether Chicano/Latino student feel respected. One possible explanation is that, at campuses with high levels of underrepresented minorities, Chicano/Latino students perceive that the presence of many Black and Chicano/Latino students signals that the campus is not selective. Conversely, at campuses with low levels of underrepresented minorities, Chicano/Latino students believe that they are at a high-quality institution.

"I feel I belong at this campus"
Black students' feelings of belonging on campus are related to the ethnic makeup of the student body. Using the percent of Black students as the measure of diversity masks the institutional factors that emerge when using categories of campuses to measure diversity. In Table 3.3,

Table 3.1: Ethnic diversity correlates of feeling respected, Black students

Predictor Variable	Model A Exp(B)		Model B Exp(B)		Model C Exp(B)		Model D Exp(B)	
Family characteristics								
Immigrant or second-generation	1.459		1.372		1.467		1.375	
Native	ref		ref		ref		ref	
Parents' income	1.144		1.088		1.112		1.114	
Mother's education	0.883		0.898		0.886		0.890	
Father's education	0.958		0.960		0.975		0.964	
Academic performance								
High school grade point average	0.915		1.654		1.094		1.235	
SAT I score	1.002	*	1.003	*	1.002	*	1.003	*
College grade point average	1.052		0.973		1.069		1.015	
Diversity measure								
Percent Black	1.424	***						
Category based on Black percent								
Lowest			ref					
Low			1.957					
High			0.982					
Highest			8.116	**				
Percent Underrep. Minority					1.109	***		

Table 3.1: Ethnic diversity correlates of feeling respected, Black students (Continued)

Predictor Variable	Model A Exp(B)		Model B Exp(B)		Model C Exp(B)		Model D Exp(B)	
Category of Underrep. Minority								
Lowest							ref	
Low							0.754	
High							0.898	
Highest							4.730	***
Constant	0.007	**	0.001	**	0.002	***	0.002	**
Number of cases	346		346		346		346	
Nagelkerke R^2	0.111		0.153		0.125		0.143	

*significant at the 0.05 level, **significant at the 0.01 level, ***significant at the 0.001 level

The notation "ref" is for the reference category of a set of variables.

Dependent variable: "Students are respected here regardless of their race or ethnicity"

Table 3.2: Ethnic diversity correlates of feeling respected, Chicano/Latino students

Predictor Variable	Model A Exp(B)		Model B Exp(B)	
Family characteristics				
Immigrant or second-generation	0.853		0.854	
Native	ref		ref	
Parents' income	1.153	**	1.135	*
Mother's education	1.074		1.062	
Father's education	1.047		1.053	
Academic performance				
High school grade point average	0.934		0.972	
SAT I score	1.001	*	1.001	
College grade point average	0.853		0.879	
Diversity measure				
Percent Underrepresented Minority	0.191	**		
Category based on percent of Underrep. Minority				
Lowest			ref	
Low			0.765	
High			0.783	*
Highest			2.076	***

Table 3.2: Ethnic diversity correlates of feeling respected, Chicano/Latino students (Continued)

Predictor Variable	Model A Exp(B)	Model B Exp(B)	
Constant		0.306	*
Number of cases	2199	2199	
Nagelkerke R^2	0.055	0.073	

*significant at the 0.05 level, **significant at the 0.01 level, ***significant at the 0.001 level

The notation "ref" is for the reference category of a set of variables.

Dependent variable: "Students are respected here regardless of their race or ethnicity"

Model A, diversity is measured in terms of the percent of Black students on campus. The representation of Black students on campus is directly and significantly related to Black students' sense of belonging. In Table 3.3, Model B, campuses are placed in categories based on the percent of Black students on campus. Black students at the most diverse campuses are 13 times more likely to feel a sense of belonging versus Black students at the least diverse campuses. Although it appears in the model presented (Table 3.3, Model B) that there is a difference between high and low diversity campuses, there is no statistical difference between these two categories of campus (model not shown). Using the percent of underrepresented minorities as the measure of diversity suggests a positive relationship to Black students' belonging (Table 3.3, Model C). When diversity is measured by categories of campuses, the idea of a critical mass of underrepresented minorities emerges. Black students at the most diverse campuses are 2.8 times more likely than Black students at the least diverse campuses to say they feel they belong at their campus (Table 3.3, Model D). The most diverse campuses are significantly different than all the other campuses, but there is no difference among campuses with the lowest, low, and high percents of underrepresented minorities (models not shown).

Binary logistic regression models of the Chicano/Latino student population show that there is no relationship between the percent of underrepresented minorities on campus and feelings of belonging (Table 3.4, Models A and B). Diversity is not a significant predictor whether measured by the percent of underrepresented minorities or using categories of campuses. Additional models comparing campus categories (low, high, and highest levels of diversity) show no difference among them. These findings suggest that, unlike Black students, diversity is not related to Chicano/Latino students' feelings of belonging on campus.

"How often have you had an in-depth conversation with students of a different race/ethnicity?"
In this section, I test the effect of diversity on interethnic interactions. For the social outcome variable measuring interethnic conversations, I present models of each ethnic group: Black, Chicano/Latino, Asian, and White. The explanatory variables are the percent of Black students

Table 3.3: Ethnic diversity correlates of belonging, Black students

Predictor Variable	Model A Exp(B)		Model B Exp(B)		Model C Exp(B)	Model D Exp(B)
Family characteristics						
Immigrant or second-generation	1.379		1.394		1.374	1.381
Native	ref		ref		ref	ref
Parents' income	1.302	*	1.280		1.278	1.277
Mother's education	0.813		0.803		0.815	0.816
Father's education	0.995		1.001		1.006	1.006
Academic performance						
High school grade point average	0.756		1.169		0.816	0.806
SAT I score	1.001		1.002		1.001	1.001
College grade point average	1.411		1.345		1.426	1.427
Diversity measure						
Percent Black	1.229	**				
Category based on Black percent						
Lowest			ref			
Low			7.413	**		
High			4.591	*		
Highest			13.196	***		
Percent Underrep. Minority					1.059 **	

Table 3.3: Ethnic diversity correlates of belonging, Black students (Continued)

Predictor Variable	Model A Exp(B)		Model B Exp(B)		Model C Exp(B)		Model D Exp(B)	
Category of Underrep. Minority								
Lowest							ref	
Low							1.276	
High							1.511	
Highest							2.880	**
Constant	0.046	*	0.003	***	0.025	*	0.055	*
Number of cases	348		348		348		348	
Nagelkerke R²	0.084		0.121		0.025		0.086	

*significant at the 0.05 level, **significant at the 0.01 level, ***significant at the 0.001 level

The notation "ref" is for the reference category of a set of variables.

Dependent variable: "I feel I belong at this campus"

Table 3.4: Ethnic diversity correlates of belonging, Chicano/Latino students

Predictor Variable	Model A Exp(B)		Model B Exp(B)	
Family characteristics				
Immigrant or second-generation	1.037		1.029	
Native	ref		ref	
Parents' income	0.967		0.967	
Mother's education	1.070		1.072	
Father's education	1.078		1.078	
Academic performance				
High school grade point average	1.019		0.994	
SAT I score	1.000		1.000	
College grade point average	1.226	*	1.227	*
Diversity measure				
Percent Underrepresented Minority	1.006			
Category based on percent of Underrep. Minority				
Lowest			ref	
Low			1.142	
High			0.999	
Highest			1.129	

Table 3.4: Ethnic diversity correlates of belonging, Chicano/Latino students (Continued)

Predictor Variable	Model A Exp(B)	Model B Exp(B)
Constant	0.552	0.671
Number of cases	2192	2192
Nagelkerke R^2	0.012	0.013

*significant at the 0.05 level, **significant at the 0.01 level, ***significant at the 0.001 level

The notation "ref" is for the reference category of a set of variables.

Dependent variable: "I feel I belong at this campus"

on campus, category of campus based on the share of Black students, percent of underrepresented minorities on campus, and category of campus based on the share of underrepresented minorities. An important factor to keep in mind for these analyses is that the relative number of co-ethnic students affects the probability that a student will encounter a student of another ethnicity. That is, Black students are simply more likely to have interethnic interactions because there are few Black students on campus. Whereas, Asian students are less likely to have interethnic interactions because there are many Asian students on campus.diversity does not have a significant effect on the frequency of Black students' engagement in interethnic conversations. The percent of Black students on campus is not related to how frequently Black students have in-depth conversations with a student of a different ethnicity (Table 3.5, Model A). In addition, campus categories based on the share of Black students was not significant in the model (Table 3.5, Model B). The results are the same when considering diversity as levels of underrepresented minorities on campus. Table 3.5 shows the models predicting interethnic conversations using the percent of underrepresented minorities on campus (Model C) and categories of campuses based on the share of underrepresented minorities (Model D). None of the measures of diversity is significantly related to the frequency of Black students' interethnic conversations.

For Chicano/Latino students, the relationship between diversity and interethnic conversations appears paradoxical. There is an inverse relationship between diversity and Chicano/Latino students' interethnic interactions, regardless of whether diversity is measured by representation of Black students (Table 3.6, Models A and B) or underrepresented minorities (Table 3.6, Models C and D) on campus. Table 3.6, Model B has categories of campuses based on the representation of Black students and campuses with the highest percentages of Black students are the reference category. Chicano/Latino students at campuses with the lowest levels and low levels of Black students are more likely to have interethnic conversations when compared to Chicano/Latino students at campuses with the highest levels of Black students. As campus diversity increases, Chicano/Latino students' frequency of interethnic conversations decreases.

The results for Asian students are similar to those for Chicano/Latino students. There is some evidence that higher levels of diversity, as measured by the percent of Black students on campus, increases, is related to lower levels of Asian students' interethnic conversations (Table 3.7, Model A). However, the results based on campus categories shows a more complex relationship. Compared with Asian students at campuses with the highest representation of Black students, Asians at campuses with the lowest and with low levels of diversity have more interethnic interaction (Table 3.7, Model B). Models C and D test the relationship between levels of underrepresented minorities on campus and Asian students' interethnic conversations. The percent of underrepresented minorities is not a significant factor (Table 3.7, Model C), however the campus categories reveal some difference by level of underrepresented minorities. Compared with Asian students at campuses with the highest levels of underrepresented minorities, Asian students at campuses with a high level of diversity are more likely to branch out of their ethnic group. This finding, along with the results based on representation of Black students, is counterintuitive and suggests that while diversity has some part in Asian students' interethnic interactions, there are other institutional factors at play.

Examining the models predicting White students' interethnic conversations, I find some evidence that ethnic diversity on campus increases interethnic interaction. There is a significant positive relationship between the percent of Black students on campus and the frequency of White students' interethnic conversations (Table 3.8, Model A). When the campuses are in groups based on their share of Black students, White students at campuses with a high level of diversity are 1.2 times more likely to have frequent conversations with a student of another ethnicity, versus White students at campuses with the lowest levels of Black students (Table 3.8, Model B). However, these results are equivocal because the odds ratio is reversed for White students at campuses with low diversity and not significant for White students at campuses with the most diversity, where we would expect the effect to be significant. The other measure of diversity is based on underrepresented minorities. The percent of underrepresented minorities on campus is not significantly related to White students' interethnic interactions (Table 3.8, Model C), but when campuses are put into categories based on their share of underrepresented minorities, some significant differences emerge. As shown in Table 3.8, Model D, White students at institutions with the highest levels of underrepresented minorities are 1.4 times more likely to have in-depth conversations with students of different ethnicities when compared to White students at institutions with the least diversity. The lack of significance when comparing the least diverse campuses with high diversity campuses underscores the importance of institutional factors. This nuance is missed in the model using the simple percentage of underrepresented minorities as the explanatory variable. Thus, the share of underrepresented minorities on campus has some effect on White students' interethnic interactions. In addition, there are other campus-level factors that account for the frequency of White students' interethnic interactions.

Summary of effects of diversity on student experience
There is a direct and significant relationship between diversity and Black students feeling respected. This holds true whether diversity is measured by the share of Black students on campus or underrepresented minorities. The results of models using categories of campus diversity suggest that reaching a certain level of diversity is related to high rates of Black students feeling respected. This supports the idea that a critical mass of co-ethnics or other ethnic minorities can affect how Black students experience their campus.

Further evidence of this relationship is given by the models predicting Black students' sense of belonging on campus. However it is measured, diversity is strongly and positively related to Black students' sense of belonging. The models using categories of campus diversity show greater effects at the highest level of campus diversity, suggesting that a critical mass of Black students or underrepresented minorities augments Black students' college experience. Neither of these social outcomes varies by immigrant generation, suggesting that Black students' experiences are common across differing histories of family immigration. A common Black student experience, regardless of immigrant, second-generation, or native status, emerged from the analysis.

Table 3.5: Ethnic diversity correlates of interethnic conversations, Black students

Predictor Variable	Model A Exp(B)	Model B Exp(B)	Model C Exp(B)	Model D Exp(B)
Family characteristics				
Immigrant or second-generation	1.060	1.044	1.062	1.044
Native	ref	ref	ref	ref
Parents' income	1.021	1.006	1.014	1.006
Mother's education	1.073	1.075	1.073	1.075
Father's education	0.973	0.975	0.972	0.975
Academic performance				
High school grade point average	0.547	0.680	0.564	0.680
SAT I score	1.002 *	1.002 *	1.002 *	1.002 *
College grade point average	1.340	1.289	1.345	1.289
Diversity measure				
Percent Black	0.987			
Category based on Black percent				
Lowest		ref		
Low		1.621		
High		1.085		
Highest		1.376		
Percent Underrep. Minority			1.005	

Table 3.5: Ethnic diversity correlates of interethnic conversations, Black students (Continued)

Predictor Variable	Model A Exp(B)	Model B Exp(B)	Model C Exp(B)	Model D Exp(B)
Category of Underrep. Minority				
Lowest				ref
Low				0.902
High				1.193
Highest				1.071
Constant	0.977	0.310	0.690	0.750
Number of cases	344	344	344	344
Nagelkerke R^2	0.040	0.047	0.041	0.043

*significant at the 0.05 level, **significant at the 0.01 level, ***significant at the 0.001 level
The notation "ref" is for the reference category of a set of variables.
Dependent variable: Frequency of in-depth conversations with a student of a different ethnicity

Table 3.6: Ethnic diversity correlates of interethnic conversations, Chicano/Latino students only

Predictor Variable	Model A Exp(B)		Model B Exp(B)		Model C Exp(B)		Model D Exp(B)	
Family characteristics								
Immigrant or second-generation	1.091		1.089		1.079		1.074	
Native	ref		ref		ref		ref	
Parents' income	0.964		0.963		0.964		0.965	
Mother's education	1.076		1.075		1.081		1.083	
Father's education	0.998		0.999		0.999		0.997	
Academic performance								
High school grade point average	0.655	**	0.646	**	0.625	***	0.617	***
SAT I score	1.001	***	1.001	***	1.001	**	1.001	**
College grade point average	1.212	*	1.218	*	1.215	*	1.214	*
Diversity measure								
Percent Black	0.933	**						
Category based on Black percent								
Lowest			1.571	*				
Low			1.333	*				
High			1.210					
Highest			ref					
Percent Underrep. Minority					0.978	**		

Table 3.6: Ethnic diversity correlates of interethnic conversations, Chicano/Latino students only (Continued)

Predictor Variable	Model A Exp(B)	Model B Exp(B)	Model C Exp(B)	Model D Exp(B)	
Category of Underrep. Minority					
Lowest				1.445	**
Low				1.502	*
High				1.232	
Highest				ref	
Constant	1.066	1.099	1.626	0.859	
Number of cases	2200	2200	2200	2200	
Nagelkerke R^2	0.029	0.030	0.030	0.030	

*significant at the 0.05 level, **significant at the 0.01 level, ***significant at the 0.001 level

The notation "ref" is for the reference category of a set of variables.

Dependent variable: Frequency of in-depth conversations with a student of a different ethnicity

Table 3.7: Ethnic diversity correlates of interethnic conversations, Asian students only

Predictor Variable	Model A Exp(B)		Model B Exp(B)		Model C Exp(B)		Model D Exp(B)	
Family characteristics								
Immigrant or second-generation	0.698	***	0.700	***	0.683	***	0.714	**
Native	ref		ref		ref		ref	
Parents' income	1.095	***	1.089	**	1.094	***	1.104	***
Mother's education	1.099	**	1.097	**	1.100	**	1.100	**
Father's education	1.063	*	1.065	*	1.059		1.056	
Academic performance								
High school grade point average	0.880		0.918		0.889		0.920	
SAT I score	0.999	**	0.999	**	0.999	**	0.999	**
College grade point average	1.078		1.073		1.064		1.056	
Diversity measure								
Percent Black	0.944	***						
Category based on Black percent								
Lowest			1.285	*				
Low			1.253	*				
High			1.077					
Highest			ref					
Percent Underrep. Minority					0.995			

Table 3.7: Ethnic diversity correlates of interethnic conversations, Asian students only (Continued)

Predictor Variable	Model A Exp(B)		Model B Exp(B)		Model C Exp(B)		Model D Exp(B)	
Category of Underrep. Minority								
Lowest							1.777	
Low							1.023	
High							1.378	**
Highest							ref	
Constant	2.452	**	1.374		2.174	*	1.422	
Number of cases	7020		7020		7020		7020	
Nagelkerke R^2	0.027		0.027		0.025		0.029	

*significant at the 0.05 level, **significant at the 0.01 level, ***significant at the 0.001 level
The notation "ref" is for the reference category of a set of variables.
Dependent variable: Frequency of in-depth conversations with a student of a different ethnicity

Table 3.8: Ethnic diversity correlates of interethnic conversations, White students only

Predictor Variable	Model A Exp(B)	Model B Exp(B)	Model C Exp(B)	Model D Exp(B)
Family characteristics				
Immigrant or second-generation	1.089	1.039	1.099	1.075
Native	ref	ref	ref	ref
Parents' income	0.997	1.015	0.991	0.987
Mother's education	0.986	0.990	0.984	0.989
Father's education	1.033	1.023	1.036	1.035
Academic performance				
High school grade point average	1.131	0.852	1.116	1.031
SAT I score	1.001 ***	1.001 *	1.001 ***	1.001 ***
College grade point average	0.911	0.951	0.922	0.943
Diversity measure				
Percent Black	1.080 ***			
Category based on Black percent				
Lowest		ref		
Low		0.609 ***		
High		1.189 *		
Highest		0.964		
Percent Underrep. Minority			1.004	

Table 3.8: Ethnic diversity correlates of interethnic conversations, White students only (Continued)

Predictor Variable	Model A Exp(B)		Model B Exp(B)		Model C Exp(B)		Model D Exp(B)	
Category of Underrep. Minority								
Lowest							ref	
Low							1.410	***
High							0.902	
Highest							1.354	**
Constant	0.219	***	1.735		0.269	***	0.417	
Number of cases	7179		7179		7179		7179	
Nagelkerke R²	0.011		0.030		0.008		0.016	

*significant at the 0.05 level, **significant at the 0.01 level, ***significant at the 0.001 level

The notation "ref" is for the reference category of a set of variables.

Dependent variable: Frequency of in-depth conversations with a student of a different ethnicity

Although some similarities to Black students are seen in the analysis on Chicano/Latino students, the relationship between diversity and college social experience is weaker and more complex. There is a positive relationship between the share of underrepresented minorities on campus and Chicano/Latino students feeling respected. However, the statistical analysis points to additional institutional explanations. There is no statistical relationship between diversity and Chicano/Latino students' sense of belonging. These results suggest that diversity is weakly related to Chicano/Latino students' college experience.

The regression analyses predicting interethnic conversations addresses a question from the literature – what is the relationship between student body diversity and interethnic interaction? Some researchers argue for increasing ethnic diversity by showing that interethnic interactions benefit students academically and socially. There is an implicit assumption that adding more Black and Chicano/Latino students to a campus increases interethnic interactions. The results from this study support this.

Ethnic diversity increases interethnic interactions for White students (Table 3.8, Model D). The models for White students lean toward the finding that diversity leads to interethnic interactions. However, the true lesson from these statistical analyses is the explanatory power of institutional factors.

Taken together, the results suggest that increasing the number of Black and Chicano/Latino students is necessary but not sufficient to increase the frequency of interethnic conversations. Across all UC campuses, 53% of students report having an in-depth conversation with a student of a different ethnicity often or very often. The remaining 47% never, rarely, or occasionally have such conversations. Clearly, there is room for improvement. Increasing the representation of ethnic minorities is a necessary step to increasing interethnic interactions, but it is not sufficient. Other institutional policies must be employed. The models presented clearly show differences by campus, emphasizing the importance of campus-level factors. Research suggests that university administrators can create opportunities for interethnic interaction. Having a roommate of a different ethnicity in a student's first year in college and participating in a celebration of another culture are positively associated with future interethnic interactions on campus (Espenshade and Radford 2009, Stearns, Buchmann, and Bonneau

2009). Research such as this can inform university policy in a nuanced way.   This particular study demonstrates that university administrators may increase interethnic interaction by encouraging events held by ethnicity-based student groups and by discouraging ethnicity-based housing for freshmen.

THE UTILITY OF RACIAL AND ETHNIC CATEGORIES FOR POLICY AND RESEARCH

The evidence from the previous section shows the importance of a sizeable representation of Black and Chicano/Latino students to Black students' social experience.   The findings are less clear about the relationship between the representation of Black and Chicano/Latino students and interethnic interactions among all students.   However, certainly students of other ethnicities must be present, and in good numbers, in order for interethnic conversations to occur.   In this section, I discuss Affirmative Action, how it relates to ethnic categories of Black students, and a glimpse into the effects of the ban on Affirmative Action programs in the UC system.

Black immigrants and Affirmative Action

Ethnic categories are important to keep track of how these groups are doing, especially given the historical and institutional racism in the United States.   Is "Black or African American" a meaningful group in terms of policy and evaluation when it is comprised of native Blacks and immigrant Blacks?   If non-Blacks in society view immigrant Blacks as native Blacks, if they are subject to the same discriminatory treatment, then for their protection and advancement, they can be categorized with native Blacks.   Since that is how society views them, they can be counted as Black or African American.

However, placing immigrant Blacks in the Black or African American category is incorrect if we are considering evaluation and policy regarding the historical discrimination of native Blacks in the United States.   If we are trying to measure the progress of native Blacks in this country, then immigrant Blacks should not be counted in the same category, especially if the educational and career outcomes of immigrant Blacks is better than that of native Blacks. In that case, the situation of native Blacks will appear to be better than what it actually is. Affirmative Action can be viewed as redress for slavery. Native Blacks have experienced many generations of discriminatory treatment, which has affected the wealth, and educational and career trajectories of contemporary native Blacks. Then only those descended from slaves should benefit from Affirmative Action. However, the current institutional racism that was created by centuries of slavery affects all Blacks in the United States. Discrimination is across all Black groups – immigrant or native.

Affirmative Action and the public university
The issue of Affirmative Action is especially relevant to public universities, such as the University of California campuses. In the late 1960's, the University of California adopted strong Affirmative Action policies, which resulted in the desegregation of its campuses (Karabel 1999). In November 1996, voters in California approved Proposition 209 which banned the consideration of race or ethnicity in, among other things, university admissions. Undergraduate applications for the UC system are due in November, so the first class that Proposition 209 affected was admitted for Fall 1998. I present data for admissions in Fall 1997 and Fall 1998 to show the effect of Proposition 209.

Before the end of Affirmative Action, 50% of African Americans who applied to UC Berkeley were admitted. After Proposition 209, only 20% of African Americans who applied to UC Berkeley were admitted (Figure 3.3). Accordingly, African American's share of all admittances decreased (Figure 3.4). Since its passage, analyses on the effect of Proposition 209 have been mixed. Some claim it is a success, redistributing low-performing students from the flagship universities to the less selective campuses, where they are more likely to succeed (Geshekter 2008). However, researchers have shown that Black students who are admitted through special programs such as Affirmative Action to elite preparatory schools (Zweigenhaft and Domhoff 1991) and selective universities (Melguizo 2008, Bowen and Bok 2000) perform well academically and go on to have successful careers. Other researchers have shown that all students benefit from interethnic interactions (Espenshade and Radford 2009, Gurin, et al. 2002, Hurtado 2005, Antonio, et al. 2004). In light of this, the marked

Figure 3.3: African American admits as a percentage of African American applicants, California residents

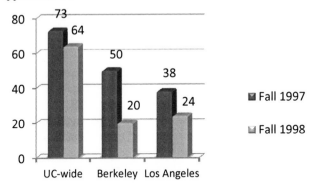

University of California, Office of the President 2003
University of California-wide, 1997 n = 2,141; 1998 n = 2,151
Berkeley, 1997 n = 1,099; 1998 n = 1,164
Los Angeles, 1997 n = 1,272; 1998 n = 1,247

Figure 3.4: African American admits as a percentage of all admits, California residents

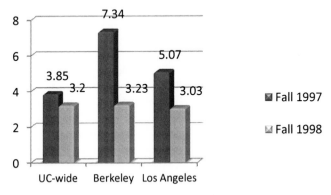

University of California, Office of the President 2003
University of California-wide, 1997 n = 40,427; 1998 n = 42,741
Berkeley, 1997 n = 7,425; 1998 n = 7,305
Los Angeles, 1997 n = 9,621; 1998 n = 9,699

decrease in the numbers of Black students admitted to the Berkeley and Los Angeles campuses (Hinrichs 2012, Ocampo 2006, Maitre 2005, Jones 1998) is disheartening.

FINDINGS FROM THE QUALITATIVE DATA

Literature on second-generation Black immigrants suggests that they will distinguish themselves from native Blacks (Vickermann 1999, Kasinitz, et al. 2008, Ogbu 1991, Deaux 2006). Waters (1999) makes the point that second-generation West Indian adolescents will make the distinction between themselves and native Blacks, while those in poor neighborhoods will be more likely to identify with native Blacks. The population in this study is more like the middle-class West Indians. And while the immigrant Black respondents in the present study see differences between themselves and native Black students, all feel some sense of belonging to a larger Black community. This finding resonates with studies of second-generation immigrants assimilating to native groups (Portes and Rumbaut 2001, Alba and Nee 2003).

Identity in college
College is an important time in identity formation. As young people live away from their natal homes and communities, they may be faced for the first time with a huge spectrum of peers from different countries, of different ethnicities, with varied orientations and viewpoints, and of different religions. The college years, the time of early adulthood when young people's careers are not yet set, are a time of identity crisis (Erikson 1968). These young adults are questioning the racial and ethnic identifiers that others have labeled them with (Chickering and Reisser 1993). They are beginning to define their identities on their own terms and with their own terms.

Sherice, a native Black student from the San Francisco Bay Area, told me that at one point, she embraced the term African American, but has since begun to question it. She said at one time, she thought, "I'm African American, I actually have an origin now." Then she learned more about Black people from other parts of the world and she explained:

The more I learn, I'm like, 'Well, actually, maybe I'm not from Africa. Maybe I'm from the Caribbean or somewhere else. I don't know where my ancestry's from. For Black people, you're trying to reclaim your roots but you don't know where they are, so you take on the, not really Americanized side of it, but you take on what you know. So, that's why I would say Black versus African American. (Sherice, native Black female, third-year student)

Sherice only really thought about immigrant Blacks when she started college and began to meet Nigerian Americans and Ethiopian Americans.

They [Black immigrants] seem like they have more values and culture. I didn't even know about all these Black immigrants until I got here. Now I'm learning about Nigerians and Ethiopians. Now I'm like, 'Wow, there are more!'... When I came here [college], I was like, 'You're Nigerian. All these Nigerians are here!' I feel like they're more culture-based. They have more values. They're more, I wouldn't say studious, but they're more determined. I guess because they have their origin. They know where they're from. They can trace back to their great-great-great-great-ancestor and stuff, versus me, I'm just an American-born Black person. I'm not sure of my roots. (Sherice)

Another native Black student described how encountering immigrant Blacks in college changed the way she thought about her own culture:

When I got here [college], I felt like I had less of a culture because they have foods and they have a language. It's a Black language and African Americans don't have a language. Their names are so specific, and I don't feel like... names that are made up have an origin and a significance like African names. That's for any culture. If it's culture-specific, it's a special name to me and I'm like, 'Wow, I wish I had a name like that or I had something I could identify with.' But we made our own culture through music and stuff, but we don't have a land of origin. It doesn't seem that special to me. (Raven, native Black female, first-year student)

Raven grew up in a racially mixed neighborhood, then attended a high school that she described as comprised of "upper-echelon Jewish white kids." These native Black students, newly exposed to immigrant Blacks, are re-thinking their culture, their origins, and their identity. Perhaps because many college students are living away from home for the first time, or because college is a time to explore one's identity, or because of the community they find themselves part of on campus, the respondents are struggling with their identity, with where to draw the lines between and around themselves.

Racial and ethnic identity of interviewees
During the interview, each interviewee was asked about their race and ethnicity. The race question was closed-ended using the census categories for race. Thirty-seven of the 39 respondents chose "Black or African American" as their race. Of that number, one immigrant Black respondent chose two categories, "Black or African American" and "Asian" because his mother is Filipino. The two respondents who did *not* choose "Black or African American" were Eniola and Itunu, immigrant Black respondents who chose "Other." These two cases are discussed in greater detail in the section that takes a closer look at "Black or African American."

The ethnicity question was open-ended. I asked each interviewee, "How would you describe your ethnicity?" and I wrote their answers on the questionnaire. Despite the great majority of the native and immigrant Black respondents identifying their *race* as Black or African American, there was no overlap in the way native Black and immigrant Black students describe their *ethnicity*.

Seventeen of the 19 native Black respondents described their ethnicity as African American and/or Black (Figure 3.5). Brandi, a native Black interviewee, said her ethnicity is "African descent." It seems that she identifies with an African origin, but her struggle with her ancestry is clear when she talked about immigrant Blacks:

They have a sense of self that I wouldn't know how to approach because they can say, 'I'm from Nigeria.' 'My family's from Curacao.' 'My family's from Dominican Republic.' And I don't really know. My mom's from Alabama. [laughs] That's what I can say. It's definitely an identity that I'm proud of, but it's not... It's slightly annoying, slightly depressing that we can't go back past the U.S. I guess if I took six months or a year, I could find out more, lots of people have. (Brandi, native Black female, first-year student)

When she talked about herself and other native Blacks during the interview, she used the term "Black."

Another native Black respondent, Robert, described his ethnicity as Jewish. He seemed unsure during the interview about his ethnicity and asked if he could say "Jewish" because he is a Christian Jew. He is not ethnically Jewish, but chose to identify as such. This is an example of how confusing racial and ethnic categories can be to survey respondents and then to researchers analyzing the data. Although he said his ethnicity was Jewish, Robert consistently used "African American" when talking about himself and other native Blacks. He could have just as easily been added to the "African American" category. Almost all of the other native Black respondents use "Black" when talking about native Blacks.

For the most part, native Black respondents identify their ethnicity as Black and/or African American. However, the native Black college students were grappling with what to call themselves and what terms to use for immigrant Blacks. The data from the questionnaires, where the native Black respondents seem to uniformly identify as Black and/or African American, belie a struggle with these terms. I will explore this struggle in the remainder of this chapter.

Since the immigrant Black respondents have families from different countries including Nigeria, Ethiopia, Eritrea, and Sudan, it is not surprising that there is variation in their ethnic identities (Table 3.9). The questionnaire shows that of the respondents whose families are from Nigeria (n = 12), most identify their ethnicity as Nigerian American (n = 7), some as Nigerian (n = 4) and one as Nigerian and

African American. It is notable that only those immigrant respondents whose families are from Nigeria use the hyphenated ethnicity "Nigerian American." The interview data shows, however, that members of other immigrant Black ethnic groups consider their identity to be hyphenated. According to the interviews, immigrant Black interviewees whose home country is Ethiopia, Eritrea, or Sudan identify with their national origin and do not use the hyphenated identity (Table 3.9). As with the native Black student data, I will show that the questionnaires do not portray the confusion immigrant Black students have about their identity, and the thought they are putting into it. The meaningfulness of the existing data on race and ethnicity of UC students and for my interviewees is contested by the findings from the interview data. College students are grappling with their racial and ethnic identity. Black college students, native and immigrant, struggle with the identifiers "Black" and "African American." Immigrant Black students may use national origin terms to identify themselves, yet feel they belong to broader racial or ethnic groups.

Figure 3.5: Ethnicity of native Black respondents (n = 19)

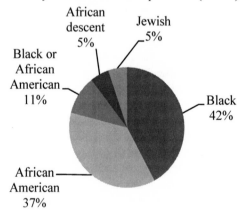

Table 3.9: Ethnicity of immigrant Black interviewees (n = 20)

Ethnicity	Number	Percent
Nigerian American	7	35
Nigerian	4	20
Ethiopian	4	20
Eritrean	2	10
Sudanese	1	5
Nigerian and African American	1	5
Ethiopian and Filipino	1	5

A closer look at "Black or African American"
The identifier African American came into the common lexicon in the 1980's as an alternative to Black. It was used in intellectual circles for years before textbooks, popular media, and the general population began to adopt it (Ogbu 2004, Wilkerson 1989). At that time, foreign-born Blacks made up less than one percent of the Black population in the United States. Not only are there more foreign-born Blacks now, but there is also a growing number of second-generation Black immigrants. The presence of immigrant Blacks in the United States has complicated the use of the term African American for my respondents. In the preface to his 1997 book The Ordeal of Integration, Orlando Patterson used the term Afro-American in place of both "Black" and "African American." More than a decade ago, Patterson saw the trend of increasing Black immigration; hence his suggestion that the term African American be reserved for those Africans who immigrate to the United States. This resonates with issues that the native Black respondents in my study have with the term African American.

The identifier African American is now being questioned, and this is perhaps most evident among Black college students. They are at a point in their lives and a place in their lives when they are thinking about their identity and have the time to do so (Erikson 1968, Chickering and Reisser 1993). The respondents in this study are on a campus that offers African American Studies classes and has Black student groups for different national origin ethnicities and to support Black students in various fields of study. As immigrant and native Black students navigate this terrain, they are probably separated from their families and placed in a community that may have a very different racial and ethnic composition than they are used to.

Respondents discussed the term African American and what it means to them. Some say that the term literally defines immigrant Blacks, although its everyday definition does not fit. That is, immigrant Blacks or their parents are from Africa and they are currently living in America, and in that way they are African American. On the other hand, the common use of the term African American is a Black person whose parents were born in the United States.

On the questionnaire for each interview, I used the standard census categories for the race question. All of the native Black respondents chose "Black or African American" as their race. This uniformity is misleading. Native Blacks are rethinking the term African American. Some respondents felt they were not entitled to the identity "African American." Since their ancestors were brought to the United States or to the former British colonies as slaves, they cannot definitively trace their ancestors to Africa. They question their claim to the term African American and some feel more comfortable identifying as Black.

One native Black respondent was reconsidering her use of the term African American, although she was one of the two native Black respondents who consistently used "African American" rather than "Black" when referring to native Blacks during her interview. Kim explained,

> I think most about being African American when I'm with Africans. Technically, they're African American too, except they can trace the African part. So sometimes I think, 'Should I just say I'm American?' I couldn't tell you what part of Africa I'm from. (Kim, native Black female, second-year student)

Taking a closer look at the term *African* American, native Black students begin to question if they can truly trace their roots to *Africa*. They know there are Black people from the Caribbean and other places, and they cannot be sure of their own family history.

Latoya, another native Black respondent lamented the fact that she doesn't feel she can claim an ethnicity. She identifies as Black:

> I say I'm Black because there can be white people from
> Africa, and they come to America and they want to be called
> African American. Our history doesn't really permit us to
> have a certain ethnicity... Just knowing about your heritage,
> knowing about your culture, where you come from, is
> different if you don't have any knowledge of that. All you
> know is oppression. If you know exactly where your parents
> are from, I think that's a gift. (Latoya, native Black female,
> second-year student)

She calls the term African American "politically correct" and "academic."

A few native Blacks discussed why they choose to identify as Black, an identifier that came into use in the United States in the 20th century. In the mid-16th century, the term Negro entered the lexicon of the territories that would become the United States of America. It was during this time period when the English entered the Atlantic slave trade, bringing African slaves to England and its colonies in North America and the West Indies (Robinson 2001). This may account for the distaste many Black Americans felt toward the identifier Negro in the 1900s, when the term colored and then Black became popular alternatives (Ogbu 2004).

As mentioned previously, almost all of the native Black respondents use "Black" (n = 17) when talking about themselves and other native Blacks during the interview. In addition, many (n = 8) of the native Black respondents explicitly identified their ethnicity as "Black." For some respondents, it is a way to claim belonging to a global Black community, as explained by Jahzara, a native Black student:

> I'm Black... I mean, there's a lot of African peoples in
> America, but then there's a lot of Black people that aren't
> necessarily from Africa and they come from the Caribbean,
> there's Black people from a lot of different places. So when I
> say Black, I identify with all Black people everywhere.
> People use them interchangeably. Whatever, African

American or Black, but if someone asks me what I am, I say, 'Black.' (Jahzara, native Black female, third-year student)

She went on to talk about the Black community on campus. Jahzara views participation in the Black community as an "obligation" for Black students because there are so few of them on campus.

Another reason that native Blacks may embrace the term Black is that they find power in it; a power that is not inherent in the term African American.

African American... it's the standard, it's the formal way. But if people ask me, I'm like, 'Oh yeah, I'm Black.' I don't have a problem with that because of, like, the Black Panther Party. There's nothing wrong with saying, 'Black power.' There's nothing wrong with it. The term African American seems too long. It takes too much out of you to say it, you know? I just like the term Black because when I hear the term Black I think of the Black Panther Party and Black pride. (Alexis, native Black female, second-year student)

Alexis described her ethnicity as African American, but used the term Black throughout the interview when talking about both immigrant and native Blacks. She did describe native Blacks as African American when distinguishing them from immigrant Blacks, for whom she used the terms second-generation or "people from Africa."

The uniformity of native Black respondents' answers to the race question masked a struggle with how to identify, and the same is true for immigrant Black respondents. Eighteen of 20 of the immigrant Black interview respondents chose "Black or African American" on the questionnaire's race question. Some are re-defining the identifier African American while others refuse it.

Forced into this racial category, some immigrant Blacks are co-opting the term "African American." Whether or not they identify with the native Black group, they define African American as *African* as in from Africa, and *American* as in living in the United States. For example, Erica, a young immigrant Black woman said, "I consider myself Eritrean, but I was born in America so I'm African American in literal terms." As with many people her age, she is struggling with her identity and to define a community that feels right for her:

> I'm part of the Ethiopian Student Union because I tried to start an Eritrean Student Union my freshmen year but it didn't work out because there's a small amount of us at Berkeley... With the Ethiopian Student Union, I don't really discriminate but we're the same kind of genre but not the same people. Most of my friends are in the ESU so that's where I feel comfortable, but other than that I wouldn't just go to an Ethiopian organization knowing that I'm Eritrean, yeah I wouldn't do that. I would love for them to change it to a Habesha Student Union, which is a branch of Ethiopians and Eritreans together, but they don't want to do that. (Erica, Eritrean female, third-year student)

Habesha is an ethnic group that is present in Ethiopia and in Eritrea, neighboring countries that were at war in the latter half of the 1900's, first over Eritrean independence then over border disputes. Erica's thoughts about how she identifies show how, even when someone identifies with a particular category, such as African American, their concept of that category may differ from the common use of the term, changing its meaningfulness. In addition, her musings on the ethnicity-based groups she choses to join demonstrate how group belonging is situational. If not for her friends in the Ethiopian Student Union, she, as an Eritrean, would not have joined an Ethiopian group. In fact, she had tried to re-name the group to fit her identity.

Nicole, a Nigerian student was explicit about feeling part of two cultures, "I think I have two different identities," she said, speaking of her Nigerian heritage and growing up in the United States. Her definition of African American is the same as Erica's:

> I am the quintessential African American because I do have direct roots in Africa but I was raised in America. I can understand that when I say I'm African American, but usually people don't think that. There's a lot of things when I'm talking to my African American friends, there's a lot of things

growing up that we don't relate on. (Nicole, identified as Nigerian and African American, first-year student)

Both of her parents emigrated from Nigeria. Nicole was born in the United States and identifies with American culture to some extent, acknowledging "two identities." Yet she feels a disconnect with native Blacks because of the differences growing up: that her parents served Nigerian food, sheltered her during her junior high and high school years, and had very high academic expectations for her. Even though most people don't recognize the term African American in the way that she uses it, she says she is the "quintessential African American."

Just as there are some immigrant Blacks who accept the term African American, another contingent (7 of 20 immigrant Blacks in the study) reject this identity. These respondents define African American as people who do not know where their ancestors are from beyond being brought over during the era of slavery in the United States. Since immigrant Blacks or their parents emigrated from Africa, they know their family's homeland.

Itunu, one of the respondents who chose "Other" for the race question during interview and specified "Nigerian," highlights the point that college and the onset of adulthood can be a time when people search for their identity. She said she used to choose "Black or African American" on forms:

> Just for people's clarity, non-Black people's clarity. They're like, 'What the difference? You're Black. You're African American, same thing.' They don't see the actual differences, so sometimes just for their convenience I just put Black or African American. But as of late, I've been putting Other, Nigerian. I feel very strongly about it. I've had many talks about the title African American. (Itunu, emigrated from Nigeria as a four-year-old, third-year student)

Itunu grew up in a closed, Nigerian community, "We did everything in our community. The kids went to high school together. They had social outings together, went to college together. It was very close." She told me how she defines African American:

I don't know how this sounds, but... to me, African Americans are people who don't have direct descendents from Africa. Literally, the ones who were brought over as slaves, centuries ago, who don't have direct relatives coming from Africa. That's what African American means to me. (Itunu)

Oladapo, an immigrant Black, chose "Black or African American" on the questionnaire, yet bristles at being called African American:

I think they should make a new category, like Nigerian American or wherever you're from... It's not correct to lump us into one category... Most people don't know that difference. They just lump us into one category of African Americans. They don't know the cultural differences. Sometimes I try to distinguish myself, not just being the typical African American. (Oladapo, Nigerian male, fourth-year student)

Oladapo was born in the U.S. but spent his childhood in Nigeria, returning to the U.S. at age 13.

Immigrant Black respondents discussed how they felt forced into a racial category for lack of a better option. They spoke of their desire to say they are Eritrean or Nigerian and their resignation at the lack of opportunity to express their ethnicity. Eniola, the other young woman who chose "Other" for race then specified "Nigerian American," explained her motivation:

I don't know what African American is... What does it mean really? African American, what is that, somewhere in Africa and then somewhere in America? Whereas I know I'm Nigerian, so why wouldn't I be specific? I'm tired of putting myself under this vague umbrella just for no purpose, when I'd just rather personally be specific. (Eniola, U.S.-born Nigerian American female, first-year student)

She talked about her family and larger Nigerian community actively preserving their Nigerian culture while in the United States. She believes it's important that the Nigerian community instills their values into her and her co-ethnic contemporaries.

There is a similar disconnect with the term "Black." Erica, the Eritrean student mentioned earlier, talked about how she thinks about her identity and that of Blacks, "I don't consider myself Black because I know where my roots, my roots go straight to somewhere, I know where I am from." (Erica, U.S.-born Eritrean female, third-year student)

A Nigerian American student, Adenike, sometimes feels compelled to be a representative for the Black community and knows she is sometimes mistaken for a native Black woman. Nonetheless she sees her ancestry as distinct from native Blacks':

> I always like to say my history doesn't entail slavery. I sympathize with the Black people because I am Black to other people, like maybe a white person might perceive me as Black. I feel like our history doesn't necessarily belong in America. Black culture has a history in America. (Adenike, U.S.-born Nigerian American, first-year student)

Adenike sees the identifier Black as belonging to native Blacks.

Native and immigrant Black students are struggling with the terms commonly used to define them – African American and Black. There appears to be a movement among them to redefine African American, which is commonly used to describe native Blacks in the United States. Some native Blacks are turning away from the term, because perhaps it more accurately defines African immigrants. During the interviews, the native Black respondents used the term "Black" when talking about other native Blacks. Some consciously embrace the term "Black" as empowering and community-building. Immigrant Blacks have split views on the term "African American." On one hand, some immigrant Blacks are co-opting the term because they feel it literally defines them, as people of African descent in America. On the other hand, some immigrant Blacks view the terms "African American" and "Black" as describing people who don't know their ancestry, and these immigrant Blacks want to be specific about where their families are from.

Ethnic identity is not absolute
Based on his large, multi-ethnic sample of young teenagers, Rubén Rumbaut (1996) found four ethnic identities that second-generation immigrants can belong to: national origin, hyphenated, assimilative unhyphenated, or dissimilative racial. Examples of these identities are, respectively: Nigerian, Nigerian American, American, or African American. He convincingly shows how each identity is linked to multiple factors, including nativity or naturalization, gender, experiences of discrimination, and the parent-child relationship.

Researchers are becoming increasingly aware of how identity is changeable over the course of one's life, dependent upon who one is being compared with, and relative to the situation (Brubaker 2009, Kasinitz, et al 2008). This is the type of fluidity and flux that I find in my respondents, even those who talk about a strong national origin identity.

When asked about ethnicity, the immigrant Black respondents cite their home country or parents' home country as their identity, as shown by the results of the questionnaire. Of the 20 immigrant Black students, 12 claimed a national origin ethnicity. For a portion of the immigrant Black students (n = 7), their ethnic identity is strong and they reject the dissimilative racial identifiers "Black" or "African American." Focusing on this contingent of immigrant Black students, I find that they still belong to native Black student groups and, in some ways, identify with native Blacks.

Itunu defined her ethnic identity by minimizing all other potential allegiances, "I feel like I'm forfeiting my title if I say I'm Nigerian American. So, I'm Nigerian. Nigerian first, and everything else after." (Itunu, Nigerian female, emigrated from Nigeria at four years old, third-year student) Yet only one of her three closest friends is Nigerian, she describes most of her friends in college as "Black," and she belongs to African American groups on campus:

> In terms of activities, a lot of my closest friends here on this campus are Black because I live here [African American Theme Program] I live with them... And then we go to the BRRC [Black Recruitment and Retention Center] meetings. And then we go to the AASC [African American Student

Council] retreat. And then we go to the NCNW [National
Council of Negro Women]. (Itunu)

Itunu was part of the Black community on campus. She acknowledged
that this is how other people see her, "At the end of the day, society
says I'm Black American. So it doesn't matter what labels we put on
ourselves. We're a community, like it or not." (Itunu) There was
resignation in her tone. Immigrant Blacks believe that white
Americans categorize them with their proximal host, native Blacks, and
this goes a long way to bringing immigrant and native Blacks into one
group. Some immigrant Blacks understand that it is in their self-
interest to work together.

Tekle, an Ethiopian student proclaimed, "I'm Ethiopian anywhere I
go. It's who I am. I'm Ethiopian, that's it." (Tekle, Ethiopian male,
immigrated to the U.S. at 11 years old, second-year student) Even this
young man who is unequivocal about his identity, is Americanized,
having spent his adolescence in Northern California. He has many
friends who recently immigrated from Ethiopia to the United States for
college. Tekle sees a difference between these young immigrants and
himself, a 1.5-generation immigrant:

> We are able to associate with our [African American] friends
> because we have more in common than they [first-generation
> immigrants] have in common with us. They don't hang out
> with people we hang out with. I'm sure that most of their
> friends are Ethiopian American, compared to us, we have both
> worlds. That's a difference I see. (Tekle)

Tekle was also immersed in the native Black community on campus.
Many of his close friends on campus were Black because of the groups
he belongs to, Biology Scholars Program and Black Students in Health
Association. He called these "support groups" and benefited greatly
from their study groups and as forums to discuss issues of minority
students in the sciences. Although he claimed a singularly Ethiopian
identity, he still differentiated himself with recently immigrated
Ethiopians and belonged to native Black groups. On some level, he is
removed from the ethnic and national group "Ethiopian." Thus,
placing second-generation Black immigrants in ethnic categories is

complex. The data from the interviews supports the view that ethnic identity is fluid and situational.

Immigrant Blacks' multiple identities
When a racial or ethnic group immigrates to the United States, the native group that society places them with has been called the proximal host (Mittelberg and Waters 1992). Native Blacks are the proximal hosts of immigrant Blacks. In this study, only five of the 39 Black college student interviewees believe that white Americans see a difference between native and immigrant Blacks. Other researchers have reported that White Americans do not perceive immigrant and native Blacks as different (Kasinitz 1992, Waters 1999, Deaux 2006). Brubaker (2009) postulates that categorization by significant others is one dimension by which a group is defined.

Becoming an undifferentiated part of the native Black group in the United States relegates immigrant Blacks to the categorical inequality that native Blacks have endured for centuries. If they completely assimilate with native Blacks, immigrant Blacks risk becoming part of a social category (with native Blacks) that is disadvantaged by institutionalized practices which allocate resources unequally (Massey 2007). Based on the existing literature on 1.5- and second-generation Black immigrants, we should expect that these respondents will clearly differentiate themselves from native Blacks. As portrayed in the interview data, immigrant Black students report that their first-generation immigrant parents are reluctant to identify with native Blacks. This reluctance is less pronounced in my mostly 1.5- and second-generation sample.

Bekele, an Ethiopian student defined "Black" as those people whose families have been in America for generations and don't have direct ties to Africa. However, he believed that the barriers between native and immigrant Blacks are very low in his generation, as opposed to his parents' cohort. He didn't struggle against the label "Black" as much as his parents do. After all, he reasoned, non-Blacks do not differentiate groups within Black:

> Because other races perceive us as one, it's not like we feel that much of a difference... There is, in my age group, there

is more unity, there's not much difference. It's not like, 'You're African, I'm Black.' (Bekele, U.S. born Ethiopian male, first-year student)

Yet Bekele identified as Ethiopian primarily. When forced to choose a racial category, he chooses African American, and thinks of it as someone of African origin in America.

Ozioma, a Nigerian American student believed that white Americans lump her into the native Black category. "If you see me in a classroom, you don't see Nigerian, you see Black," she said. She described the assumptions that she believes white Americans have about Blacks, that, "Africans are smarter, like Nigerians are smarter. I don't know where that stereotype came from. It's not a bad one, but you do hear a lot that Nigerians are smart." (Ozioma, U.S.-born Nigerian female, first-year student) Despite her belief in the existence of this positive stereotype, she does not volunteer her ethnicity. People may ask about her name because it's unique in America, and find out she's Nigerian that way, but "I don't really play the card, unless they ask."

Titilayo, another Nigerian American embraced both parts of her hyphenated identity and explained the two groups she belongs to:

I definitely feel like I'm part of the Black community. A lot of my friends are African American or Black. But just the way I've been brought up, at home speaking the language, being really involved with my parents' cultural things. We go to a lot of, especially in the summertime and even during the school year, we go to a lot of Nigerian parties, weddings, outings, baby showers. All throughout my life, I've been immersed in the culture. In high school I really did try to be involved with the Black community and the Black Student Union, I was the president of that my senior year, but from my background, I would have to say that I do identify myself as Nigerian American. (Titilayo, Nigerian female, immigrated to the U.S. at three years old, second-year student)

Amara is an immigrant Black respondent who strongly identified with being Black. She said that other people perceive her as native

Black and she is treated as a native Black. It made sense to her that immigrant Blacks join forces with native Blacks.

If someone asks me what I am, I'm like, 'Black, African American.' Unless someone's like, 'Where were you born?' then it doesn't come up. I'm like, 'I'm Black just like you. For everyone else, I look the same as you, so I'm treated just like you by society so might as well just work together.' (Amara, Ethiopian female, immigrated to the U.S. at eight years old, third-year student)

When asked if White Americans or Asians see differences within the Black community, Amara said, "They don't think about the country. They're just like, 'You're Black.'" Yet, when asked to describe her ethnicity, she said Ethiopian. Her family is an active part of the larger Ethiopian community in the Bay Area, where Amara grew up. Her parents speak to her in Amharic, which she can speak, read, and write.

The interview data show that the distinction between immigrant and native Blacks is weak for this group. Although ethnic identity emerges as fluid and situational, immigrant and native Black students count each other among their close friends, belong to the same student groups, and feel a sense of community. The composition of the Black student network will be discussed in greater detail in Chapter 4. The unity among immigrant and native Black students separates 1.5- and second-generation students from their immigrant parents who see a strong distinction between native and immigrant Blacks.

Thus, 1.5- and second-generation Black immigrants are moving toward a pan-ethnic Black identity, notably different from their immigrant parents. Previous literature has suggested that second-generation Black immigrants, particularly those who are upwardly-mobile (Waters 1999), will distance themselves from native Blacks (Ogbu 1991, Vickermann 1999, Kasinitz, et al. 2008). While some immigrant Black respondents in this study have strong national origin identities and clearly differentiate themselves from native Blacks, there is, nevertheless, a growing sense of a Black community, even among these strongly nationalistic immigrant Blacks. Waters (1999:8) studied West Indian immigrants and their children, finding that "Race as a master status in the United States soon overwhelms the identities of the immigrants and their children, and they are seen as black Americans." The qualitative data in this work resonates with Waters' findings.

DISCUSSION

This chapter began with a look at the social experiences of college students by ethnicity. I found that Black students' social experiences differed greatly from those of non-Black students. Thus, despite the presence of Chicano/Latino and Asian students on UC campuses, the color line emerges between Black and non-Black students. Also supporting this finding is the discussion of Black student identity based on the qualitative data. Immigrant and native Black students are thoughtfully considering the ethnic identifiers that are commonly used for Blacks in the U.S. They are discussing and debating these terms, who is included and excluded. On the whole, I found that there is a sense of unity among Black students. A *unique* Black college experience emerges, an experience common to Black students and different from non-Black students. The unique Black college experience likely explains the need for a critical mass of co-ethnics on campus for Black students to have a strong sense of belonging and to feel respected. This is less true for Chicano/Latino students.

In this chapter, I also explored the relationship between ethnic diversity and student outcomes. While interethnic interaction has been shown to have significant positive effects on college students of all ethnicities (Gurin, et al. 2002, Hurtado 2005, Espenshade and Radford 2009), the link between diversity and interethnic interaction has largely been assumed. I examined whether increasing diversity, measured in several ways, directly increases interethnic interaction. I found that this relationship was largely not significant.

Although the statistical relationship between diversity and interethnic interaction is not direct, it is still necessary to increase the share of underrepresented minorities on college campuses (to the point where they are no longer "underrepresented"). After all, in order to have interethnic interactions, there must be sufficient numbers of students of other ethnicities. Thus, the first step in encouraging interethnic interactions is to ensure that a critical mass of ethnic minority students is present on campus.

Since Black and Chicano/Latino college applicants, on the whole, have lower academic credentials than their White or Asian counterparts (Jencks and Phillips 1998, Espenshade and Radford 2009), race-blind admissions results in underrepresentation of Black and Chicano/Latino students. If university officials espouse a policy of ethnic diversity, then Affirmative Action is necessary.

The second step is to facilitate micro-level interactions among students of different ethnicities. One example is first-year roommate assignment to encourage interethnic roommates. It may seem paradoxical to fund and promote ethno-centric student groups in order to encourage interethnic interactions; however, there are two reasons to support such groups. The first is for the much-needed social and academic support, which is discussed in detail in Chapter 4. Secondly, ethnic events hosted by these groups introduce students of other ethnicities to different cultures. Not surprisingly, Espenshade and Radford (2009) found that students who participate in a celebration of another ethnic group have higher odds of socially interacting with that group.

CONCLUSION

In a New York Times piece Orlando Patterson (2009) defines the persistent racial problem in the United States as "at heart, a black-white issue." Even with all the immigration from Mexico, Central America, and Asia, race in the United States comes is essentially a line between Blacks and non-Blacks. However, he rightly observes that West Indian immigrants could be an exception to the disadvantageous place Blacks find themselves in the United States. The same may be said for Black immigrants from Africa, who have higher education and income levels than native Blacks. Perhaps when immigrant Blacks distance themselves socially from native Blacks and turn a blind eye to discrimination, they may singly succeed. However, nothing is done to dismantle institutional racism, or address residential segregation and educational disparities. In this environment, both native and immigrant Blacks are relegated to the bottom of the socioeconomic hierarchy.

This study is about students at a selective university, so they have all but surmounted the racial barriers around higher education. As I discuss in the chapter about educational attainment, even in this privileged environment, race and ethnicity continue to be relevant, and the significant distinction is between Black and White.

CHAPTER 4
Social Capital and Student Retention

Social integration into networks and groups on campus is an important aspect of the college student experience and can affect academic outcomes. Social capital is a concept used to articulate the resources and expectations that arise from a social relationship (Coleman 1988, Portes 1998). A college student acquires social capital by integrating into groups on campus. The social capital manifests in many ways: camaraderie, information on how to navigate campus resources, and academic support are a few examples.

The theory of social capital dovetails provides a basis for the prevailing model of college student attrition (Tinto 1975, 1993). To build his theory, Tinto drew upon Durkheim's seminal sociological work on suicide and Van Gennep's anthropological model of transitions. Tinto posits that integration into the social and intellectual life on campus will increase a student's chances of retention and eventual graduation. He argues that the more central a student group is to the mainstream culture of the campus, the more beneficial the group will be to its members.

A seminal work of modern sociology, Granovetter's (1973) theory of strong and weak ties, is the basis for Putnam's (2000) concepts of bridging and bonding social capital. I use them to frame the discussion about the college student networks, especially as they relate to underrepresented ethnic minority students. Bridging social capital results from relationships among people who differ on important characteristics. Bonding social capital arises among people with similar characteristics. For example, a Black student network can have both bonding and bridging social capital. The network *bonds* people who belong to the same pan-ethnic group: Black. Since the members share this ascriptive characteristic, they may be able to empathize with and support each other. In addition, the network *bridges* across diverse backgrounds since immigrant and native Black students or students of different social classes may be brought together in this network. Bridging social capital can generate a broader identity for Black students of disparate backgrounds.

Social capital and educational outcomes
Although it is not the main thrust of his work, Putnam (2000) addresses social capital in schools (mainly elementary schools and the communities that surround them). He suggests that the *presence* of social capital is a crucial factor determining academic outcomes; whether it is bridging or bonding social capital is important, but ultimately of less consequence than the richness of the network. There are two questions that are salient to the present study: Is social capital a significant predictor of educational outcomes? And, do outcomes depend upon *bridging* social capital?

The first empirical issue I address in this chapter is the relationship between social integration and educational outcomes for students of different ethnicities. Tinto's (1975) theory of college attrition applies the concept of social capital to the college campus: students who are engaged in college organizations are more likely to continue enrollment and to graduate. Some researchers have found that social integration is important to Hispanic and Native American student retention (Murguia, Padilla, and Pavel 1991). However, in studies of Black college students, researchers report that social integration is not related to college grade point average (Allen 1992) nor to persistence in college (Mallinckrodt 1988). These studies question the relevance of Tinto's theory to Black students.

The second line of inquiry addresses the type of social capital that students can have. Some researchers have found that certain paths of social integration are more beneficial in terms of academic, psychological, and social outcomes. Allen (1985) describes "interpersonally accomplished" Black students who maintain good relationships with co-ethnics and people of other ethnicities, and with faculty and students. This type of student is similar to Carter's (2005) cultural straddlers. Cultural straddlers belong to networks with bridging *and* bonding social capital, easily switching between co-ethnic and interethnic communities. Students with bridging social capital in particular are better poised to achieve academically.

Social capital in the Black student community

Scholarly work on foreign-born Blacks and their children has shown that they distance themselves socially from native Blacks (Kasinitz, et al. 2008). Other research shows how social closeness is situational. As discussed in Chapter 3, Waters (1992) demonstrates the effect of discrimination on the ethnic identities of West Indian immigrants and second-generation immigrants. Those who were middle-class and upwardly mobile were more likely to hold onto their ethnic identifiers. Poor and working-class West Indian immigrants who came up against racial discrimination were more likely to begin identifying as Black Americans. Smith and Moore (2000) found that Black students with immigrant backgrounds were socially close to native Black students. Is there a unified Black student community, bridging the divide between immigrant and native Blacks? The qualitative component of the present study adds to the debate by examining the groups to which immigrant versus native Black students at one campus belong.

Interview respondents discussed the student networks they belonged to. Three paths of social integration emerged from the interview data. I call them "paths" because they represent processes of integration rather than an end or static state. For example, some students ensconce themselves in the Black community on campus then abandon that network for another, such as an ethnically-diverse fraternity. There is a marked fluidity in the social structures of these college students. Nevertheless, I distill three paths: embedded in the Black community on campus, anchored in the Black community but branching out, and outside the Black community. I describe these typologies and give examples of them. I also present respondents' narratives explaining their chosen path to social integration on campus.

The interview data provide a rich description of the support students derive from the Black student community. Although scholarly work has shown the social and psychological benefits of the Black community on college campuses (Museus 2008, Murguia, Padilla, and Pavel 1991, Price, Hyle, and Jordan 2009), few delve into the academic effects of these communities (an exception is Mallinckrodt 1988). The gap may be due to the lack of a statistical relationship between social capital and academic outcomes for Black students (Mallinckrodt 1988, Allen 1992). The present study contributes to the literature by using qualitative data to detail the academic benefits of social capital that bonds Black students.

The qualitative findings thus describe Black students at one campus in terms of: (1) the composition of the Black student community, specifically as it relates to native and immigrant Blacks, (2) the different paths of social integration that emerged from the interviews, and (3) the support students find in the Black network on campus.

RESULTS FROM THE STATISTICAL DATA

Social integration
The measure of social integration I use for analysis is based upon two different aspects of student social life: (1) weekly time spent on a student group and (2) belonging to a student group. For the first variable, students were asked how much time per week they spent on "student clubs or groups such as publications, cultural groups, or student government." Answers ranged from zero to more than 17 hours per week. In order to make a distinction between students who participated in student groups and those who did not, I divided the respondents (n = 43,124) into those who spent some time on student clubs each week (49.5%) and those who reported spending zero hours on student clubs each week (50.5%).

For the second variable, students were asked if they were a part of certain types of student groups. Respondents (n = 51,819) indicated whether they were officers/leaders or members/participants in four separate categories: student government, fraternity/sorority, university-sponsored intercollegiate athletic team, or other campus-based club or organization. The resulting values were: belonging (41.5%) or not belonging (58.5%).

Thus, the variable measuring social integration is a combination of *two* variables: weekly time spent on a student group and belonging to a student group (Figure 4.1). Respondents (n = 48,049) who spent time weekly on a student group *or* who belonged to a student group were considered integrated (62.7%). Those who did neither were called not integrated (37.3%). Examination of this social integration variable by ethnicity is shown in Figure 4.2. Black and Asian students are more socially integrated than White and Chicano/Latino students.

Figure 4.1: Creation of the social integration variable

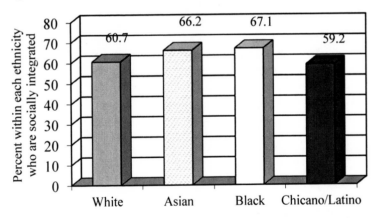

Weekly time spent on student group		Belonging to a student group	Social integration variable
1-17 hours	OR	Leader or member	→ **Integrated**
0 hours	AND	Not a leader or member	→ **Not integrated**

Figure 4.2: Social integration by ethnicity (n = 43,326)

Social integration is a dichotomous variable created from two variables: (1) Weekly time spent on student clubs or groups such as publications, cultural groups, or student government and (2) Leadership or participation in student government, fraternity/sorority, university-sponsored intercollegiate athletic team or other campus-based club or organization. Those who are counted as socially integrated spent some time on student groups weekly and/or belonged to a student group. There is a significant relationship between ethnicity and social integration (chi-square with 3 degrees of freedom, significance = 0.000).

Bridging social capital

I measure bridging social capital in terms of frequency of interethnic conversations. One question on the UCUES 2004 asked the frequency of in-depth conversations with students of a different ethnicity. Respondents chose answers from a closed set of five choices, ranging from "Never" to "Very Often." A little over half (53.1%) of UC students (n = 42,395) report having in-depth conversations often or very often with students of a different ethnicity.

As noted in Chapter 3, the relative number of co-ethnic students on campus greatly affects the probability that a student will encounter, and thus, interact with a student of another ethnicity. In addition, the definition of an "in-depth conversation" varies. For example, a Black student who is unaccustomed to being around Asians may construe a superficial conversation as in-depth, while a Black student who is grew up in an ethnically diverse neighborhood might define the same interaction as small talk.

Black students are more likely than students of other ethnicities to report having an in-depth conversation often or very often with students of a different ethnicity (Figure 4.3). There is no difference between immigrant and native Black students (not significant at the 0.05 level, n = 863). Asian students are the least likely to report having an in-depth conversation with students of a different ethnicity. It is much harder, in terms of absolute numbers, for Black students to remain socially segregated. Black students are a small proportion of UC students (less than 5%). Asian and White students are each over one-third of the UC population, and Latinos make up over 10% of the student body.

CORRELATES OF SOCIAL INTEGRATION

The preceding statistical results suggest that social integration into college differs by ethnicity. The importance of the institution in students' social experiences emerged from the statistical analyses in Chapter 3. This section has three models predicting social integration of different populations: the full UC population, Black UC students, and respondents at the interview site only. The dependent variable is social integration, as described in the preceding section. Odds ratios, Exp(B), based on binary logistic regression are given in the following models.

Figure 4.3: Frequency of in-depth conversations with students of a different ethnicity, by ethnicity (n = 38,229)

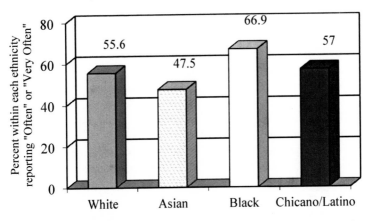

Question "How often do you have in-depth conversations with students of a different ethnicity?"
Black students' responses are different from other ethnicities (Chi-square significance at the 0.001 level). The proportion of each ethnicity on campus affects the results of these statistics. The definition of "in-depth conversations" may vary.

In the first set of regression models (Table 4.1), all UC students are included. As seen in the crosstabulation of social integration and ethnicity (Figure 4.2), Black and Asian students are more socially integrated than White students (reference category). Immigrants and second-generation immigrants are more likely to be socially integrated than natives. Both mother's and father's education have positive effects of social integration, even after high school and college factors are added (Table 4.1, Models 3a and 3b). High school and college academic performance are directly and significantly related to social integration.

Two models test institutional effects in different ways. There is no direct relationship between campus diversity (campuses grouped by their proportion of underrepresented minorities) and social integration. However, the results show the importance of other institutional factors. That is, diversity is not directly related to social integration, but some campus categories are significant (Table 4.1, Model 3a), suggesting that campuses differ in their students' levels of social integration. Another way to group institutions is by campus selectivity, using the average SAT I score and high school grade point average of the incoming freshmen class. When campuses are grouped by selectivity, it becomes clear that students at flagship and competitive campuses are more socially integrated than the students at less competitive campuses (Table 4.1, Model 3b). Further analysis (not shown) indicates that students at the flagship campuses are 1.5 times more likely to be socially integrated than students at competitive campuses. Thus, the selectivity of the campus affects social integration.

The mechanism by which selectivity and social integration are related may be due to some quality in the student body that is differentially distributed by campus selectivity or to institutional resources that are related to selectivity. Those matriculating to selective universities may be more likely to join student groups than those matriculating to less selective campuses. Also, campus endowments are related to their selectivity. The flagship campuses have very large endowments in comparison to the other campuses. More than 75% of the total amount of endowments for the eight campuses belonged to the two flagship campuses. Only about 3% belonged to the less competitive campuses. This data is from 2004, the year the UCUES data was collected (UC Annual Endowment Report, 2004). Endowments can be used to fund undergraduate scholarships and student services, which effect students' social integration. Another factor to consider is that less competitive UC campuses are more likely to have commuter students. Thus, social integration could be related to whether students live on campus or at home.

Looking at the model for Black UC students (Table 4.2), one factor is clearly significant: the institution. I tested institutional effects in two ways: grouping campuses by proportion of the student body that is Black (Table 4.2, Model 3a) and by selectivity (Table 4.2, Model 3b). Similar to the model with all UC students, Black UC students at more selective campuses are more socially integrated than students at the less competitive colleges. There is no difference in the social integration of students at flagship versus competitive campuses (model not shown).

Table 4.1: Binary logistic regression predicting social integration, all UC students

Predictor Variable	Model 1 Exp(B)		Model 2 Exp(B)		Model 3a Exp(B)		Model 3b Exp(B)	
Background characteristics								
Immigrant or second-generation	1.199	***	1.198	***	1.187	***	1.145	***
Native	ref		ref		ref		ref	
Female	1.082	***	1.100	***	1.075	***	1.060	**
Male	ref		ref		ref		ref	
Black	1.452	***	1.474	**	1.503	**	1.356	*
Chicano/Latino	1.166	***	1.126	**	1.144	***	1.091	*
Asian	1.311	***	1.211	***	1.235	***	1.208	***
White								
Mother's education	1.099	***	1.086	***	1.085	***	1.090	***
Father's education	1.089	***	1.064	***	1.065	***	1.065	***
Parents' income	1.054	***	1.029	**	1.025	**	1.047	***
High school factors								
High school grade point average			1.597	***	1.346	***	1.057	
SAT I score			1.000	**	1.000		0.999	***
College factors								
College grade point average					1.212	***	1.258	***

Table 4.1: Binary logistic regression predicting social integration, all UC students (Continued)

Predictor Variable	Model 1 Exp(B)		Model 2 Exp(B)		Model 3a Exp(B)		Model 3b Exp(B)	
Category of Underrep. Minority								
Lowest					ref			
Low					1.160	***		
High					0.987			
Highest					0.766	***		
Campus selectivity								
Flagships							2.357	***
Competitive							1.582	***
Less competitive							ref	
Constant	0.772	***	0.129	***	0.209	***	0.457	***
Number of cases	21,431		17,208		17,208		17,208	
Nagelkerke R²	0.022		0.027		0.031		0.044	

*significant at the 0.05 level, **significant at the 0.01 level, ***significant at the 0.001 level
The notation "ref" is for the reference category of a set of variables.
Dependent variable Social Integration is a combination of weekly time spent on student groups and membership in student groups (Figure 4.1).

As with the model that included all ethnicities, the relationship between diversity and social integration is complex. Compared with the campuses with the highest proportions of Black students, Black students at all other campuses are *more* likely to be socially integrated (Table 4.2, Model 3a). There is no statistical difference among the campuses with the lowest, low, and high representation of Black students (models not shown).

The effect of socioeconomic status, which was straightforwardly positive in the previous model with all ethnicities, is unclear in the model with only Black students. Although father's education is positively related, income has a negative effect. Lastly, immigrant generation is not a significant predictor of social integration for Black students; again, this finding is different from the model with all ethnicities. These differences suggest that social integration of Black students versus non-Black students is affected by different factors.

CORRELATES OF BRIDGING SOCIAL CAPITAL

I used binary logistic regression to determine the predictors of students' frequency of interethnic conversations. The frequency of interethnic interactions is related to the ethnic diversity of the campus. The results are displayed in odds ratios, Exp(B). The dependent variable is described in the preceding section and I dichotomized the answers so the two values are "Very Often" and "Often" versus "Sometimes," "Rarely," and "Never." This recoding is meant to contrast those students who have a network of interethnic friends (those they have in-depth conversations with often) versus those whose networks are mostly co-ethnic.

Other empirical work has shown a relationship between socioeconomic status and bridging social capital. Espenshade and Radford (2009) a negative correlation between social class and interacting with students of other ethnicities. Other works are able to differentiate between White and Black students. That is, White students and Black students from more advantageous class backgrounds are less likely to have networks that include minority students. For White students, high socioeconomic status is related to networks that bond with other White students. And for Black students,

Table 4.2: Binary logistic regression predicting social integration, Black UC students

Predictor Variable	Model 1 Exp(B)		Model 2 Exp(B)		Model 3a Exp(B)		Model 3b Exp(B)	
Background characteristics								
Immigrant or second-generation	1.275		1.001		1.017		1.000	
Native	ref		ref		ref		ref	
Female	0.843		1.082		1.127		1.063	
Male	ref		ref		ref		ref	
Mother's education	1.015		1.048		1.031		1.021	
Father's education	1.141		1.277		1.325	*	1.300	*
Parents' income	0.766	*	0.690	**	0.715	*	0.726	*
High school factors								
High school grade point average			1.246		0.659		0.690	
SAT I score			1.001		1.000		1.000	
College factors								
College grade point average					1.541		1.560	
Category based on percent Black								
Lowest					5.597	**		
Low					2.902	**		
High					3.269	**		
Highest					ref			

Table 4.2: Binary logistic regression predicting social integration, Black UC students (Continued)

Predictor Variable	Model 1 Exp(B)	Model 2 Exp(B)	Model 3a Exp(B)	Model 3b Exp(B)
Campus selectivity				
Flagships				.712 *
Competitive				.819 *
Less competitive				ref
Constant	3.205 **	0.465	2.034	1.465
Number of cases	444	350	350	350
Nagelkerke R^2	0.024	0.045	0.119	0.105

*significant at the 0.05 level, **significant at the 0.01 level, ***significant at the 0.001 level

The notation "ref" is for the reference category of a set of variables.

Dependent variable Social Integration is a combination of weekly time spent on student groups and membership in student groups (Figure 4.1).

this means that high socioeconomic status is related to networks that bridge ethnic divides. This may be the product of non-Black pre-college environments of Blacks from higher socioeconomic classes (Stearns, Buchmann, and Bonneau 2009).

Table 4.3 shows the models with the full UC population. As suggested by the crosstabulation depicted in Figure 4.3, Black and Chicano/Latino students are more likely than White students to engage in frequent interethnic conversations, while Asian students are less likely (Table 4.3, Models 1 through 3). The models also show that, taking other background characteristics as well as high school and college factors into account, female students are 1.2 times more likely than male students to have frequent interethnic conversations (Table 4.3, Model 3). Socioeconomic status is significantly related to interethnic conversations. The effect of socioeconomic status on interethnic conversations should be interpreted with caution. This variable may operate differently based on ethnicity. That is, Black students with high socioeconomic status may be more likely to engage in interethnic conversations with White students, while White students with high socioeconomic status may be more likely to engage in interethnic conversations with Asians. The variable measuring frequency of interethnic conversations does not give any information about the ethnicity of the student with whom the respondent is having conversations. Also notable is the non-significance of diversity, which is represented by campuses grouped by their proportion of underrepresented minorities (Table 4.3, Model 3).

The regression using only Black UC students was presented in Chapter 3 to illustrate the effect of campus diversity on interethnic interactions. Looking back on that model in Chapter 3 (Table 3.5), the only significant predictor of Black students' frequency of interethnic conversations is SAT I score. The magnitude of the coefficient is almost zero, suggesting that the variable does not greatly affect interethnic interactions. As with the regression model predicting social capital, this one predicting interethnic interactions of Black students suggests that social integration of Black students is different than social integration of students of other ethnicities.

Table 4.3: Binary logistic regression predicting interethnic conversations, all UC students

Predictor Variable	Model 1 Exp(B)		Model 2 Exp(B)		Model 3 Exp(B)	
Background characteristics						
Immigrant or second-generation	0.982		0.978		0.976	
Native	ref		ref		ref	
Female	1.148	***	1.198	***	1.200	***
Male	ref		ref		ref	
Black	1.709	***	1.821	***	1.815	***
Chicano/Latino	1.262	***	1.270	***	1.271	***
Asian	0.782	***	0.767	***	0.763	***
White	ref		ref		ref	
Mother's education	1.083	***	1.057	**	1.057	**
Father's education	1.046	*	1.039	*	1.040	*
Parents' income	1.037	*	1.033	*	1.032	
High school factors						
High school grade point average			0.901	*	0.891	*
SAT I score			1.001	***	1.001	***
College factors						
College grade point average					1.004	

Table 4.3: Binary logistic regression predicting interethnic conversations, all UC students (Continued)

Predictor Variable	Model 1 Exp(B)		Model 2 Exp(B)		Model 3 Exp(B)	
Category of Underrep. Minority						
Lowest					ref	
Low					1.003	
High					0.957	
Highest					0.982	
Constant	0.738	***	0.626	*	0.666	
Number of cases	20,823		16,743		16,743	
Nagelkerke R²	0.022		0.023		0.023	

*significant at the 0.05 level, **significant at the 0.01 level, ***significant at the 0.001 level
The notation "ref" is for the reference category of a set of variables.
Dependent variable is frequency of in-depth conversations with a student of a different ethnicity.

Social capital and educational outcomes

The variable under investigation is a dichotomous measure of graduation versus non-enrollment in 2007 for all students enrolled in a UC in 2004. The models are binary logistic regressions and the results are shown in odds ratios, Exp(B). The measure for institutional effects is campus selectivity, since the selectivity of the campus is an important factor in graduation (Gansemer-Topf and Schuh 2006, Melguizo 2008).

In the model with all UC students (Table 4.4), I first test the effect of background variables on graduation. Female students are 1.3 times more likely to graduate than male students. Socioeconomic status has a positive effect, as seen by the direct and significant effect of father's education. Black and Chicano/Latino students are less likely to graduate than White students (reference category), while Asian students are 1.2 times more likely to graduate.

Adding pre-college academic performance does not change the significance of the background variables very much (Table 4.4, Model 2), and high school grade point average and SAT I score are, in themselves, important predictors of college graduation. The next model adds an institutional variable: campus selectivity (Table 4.4, Model 3). This is an important factor predicting graduation. As expected, the more selective the college, the more likely students are to graduate.

To test if there is a relationship between bridging social capital and graduation, I added the variable measuring the frequency of interethnic conversations (Table 4.4, Model 4a). Bridging social capital does not appear to have a significant effect on graduation. To examine the relationship between the *presence* of social capital and graduation, I added the variable measuring social integration (Table 4.4, Model 4b). Adding the social integration variable doesn't change the significance of the variables from the previous model, but social integration is significantly related to graduation. The causal relationship between participation in campus groups and graduation is not clear. If a student is doing well in school, she may be more likely to join campus groups. If a student is involved in campus groups, that could benefit her academically. It is likely that there is a reciprocal relationship

Table 4.4: Social capital correlates of continued enrollment and graduation, all UC students

Predictor Variable	Model 1 Exp(B)	Model 2 Exp(B)	Model 3 Exp(B)	Model 4a Exp(B)	Model 4b Exp(B)
Background characteristics					
Immigrant or second-generation	1.012	1.057	1.036	1.044	1.030
Native	ref	ref	ref	ref	ref
Female	1.328 ***	1.238 **	1.228 ***	1.231 ***	1.233 ***
Male	ref	ref	ref	ref	ref
Black	0.456 ***	0.697 *	0.664 **	0.660 **	0.654 **
Chicano/Latino	0.620 ***	0.760 **	0.746 **	0.736 **	0.747 **
Asian	1.211 *	1.226 *	1.224 *	1.221 *	1.215 *
White	ref	ref	ref	ref	ref
Mother's education	0.990	0.984	0.992	0.990	0.988
Father's education	1.110 ***	1.069 *	1.074 *	1.077 *	1.071 *
Parents' income	1.045	1.043	1.056	1.055	1.052

Table 4.4: Social capital correlates of continued enrollment and graduation, all UC students (Continued)

Predictor Variable	Model 1 Exp(B)		Model 2 Exp(B)		Model 3 Exp(B)		Model 4a Exp(B)		Model 4b Exp(B)	
High school factors										
High school grade point average			4.109	**	3.346	***	3.332	***	3.329	***
SAT I score			1.000	*	1.000	*	1.000		1.000	
Campus selectivity										
Flagships					1.690	***	1.683	***	1.611	***
Competitive					1.394	***	1.392	***	1.356	***
Less competitive					ref		ref		ref	
Social capital variables										
Interethnic conversations							1.049			
Social integration									1.293	***
Constant	5.253	***	0.017	**	0.039	**	0.035	***	0.035	***
						*				
Number of cases	20,519		16,748		16,748		16,617		16,694	
Nagelkerke R^2	0.024		0.084		0.088		0.190		0.089	

*significant at the 0.05 level, **significant at the 0.01 level, ***significant at the 0.001 level. The notation "ref" is for the reference category of a set of variables.

between social integration and college academic performance. Consistent with Tinto's model (1993), I found a link between a student's social integration on campus and his likelihood of graduating.

Next, I ran regressions with the same variables but different populations based on ethnicity: Black students, Chicano/Latino students, Asian students, and White students. These models allow me to determine the significance of these variables to each ethnic group; the significant predictors *do* vary by ethnicity.

In the models on Black students (Table 4.5), only high school grade point average predicts graduation. Immigrant generation is not a significant factor in Black student graduation rates, which I discuss at length in Chapter 6. Neither social integration nor interethnic conversations is related to graduation for Black students (Table 4.5, Models 4a and 4b). This resonates with previous research (Tauriac and Liem 2012, Allen 1992) that academic performance is decoupled from social involvement on campus for Black students at predominantly White institutions. A possible explanation is that Black student networks may exist on the periphery of the campus social life (Tinto 1993). Integration into such a network will not yield the benefits of integration into the social mainstream of the campus, which was demonstrated in the model that included all UC students (Table 4.4, Model 4b). In terms of interethnic conversations, the lack of specificity in this variable is problematic when attempting to interpret the results. It is not possible to tell the ethnicity of the student with whom the respondent is interacting. Thus, interactions with White students are indistinguishable from interactions with Chicano/Latino students.

For Chicano/Latino students, high school grade point average predicts graduation throughout all models where it is included (Table 4.6, Models 2 through 4b). The institution is also important. Campus selectivity is directly related to graduation, at least when comparing flagship campuses with less competitive campuses. Bridging social capital, as measured by interethnic conversations, is significantly related to graduation (Table 4.6, Model 4b).

In the models with Asian students only, female students are more likely than males to graduate from college (Table 4.7). This background variable remains significant and the magnitude constant regardless of the addition of other variables. One measure of socioeconomic background, father's education, predicts graduation, but is no longer significant once high school factors are taken into account (Table 4.7, Model 2). This suggests that the benefit of paternal educational attainment is recognized in high school. Both high school performance and campus selectivity are significantly related to graduation. As with the Black student models, social integration and interethnic conversations are not significantly related to graduation (Table 4.7, Models 4a and 4b).

For White students, socioeconomic status, as measured by father's education, is a significant predictor of graduation across all models (Table 4.8). This is not true for any other ethnic group. Similar to the models based on other ethnicities, high school academic performance is significantly related to graduation. As with the Chicano/Latino and Asian models, campus selectivity predicts graduation (Table 4.8, Model 3) and the benefit of selectivity extends beyond the flagship campuses. In addition to students at flagship campuses, White students at competitive campuses are more likely to graduate compared to their peers at less competitive campuses. For White students, there is a direct, significant relationship of social integration to graduation (Table 4.8, Model 4b).

In these models on ethnic group populations, the relationship between social capital and graduation is not assumed to be unidirectional. Social integration and graduation are significantly related for White and Chicano/Latino students. College persistence and participation in on-campus groups influence each other, rather than one causing the other.

Across all populations, high school grade point average is the most consistent predictor of graduation. This is not surprising since those who excelled in high school are likely to continue to do well in college (Hershberger and D'Augelli 1992). Other correlates of educational outcomes vary by ethnicity. Attempts to fit one model of college attrition across students of different ethnicities will miss crucial differences among these groups. For example, the prevailing model of student attrition (Tinto 1975, 1993) has social integration at its core. Although social integration is significant in the model that includes all ethnicities and the models for Chicano/Latino and for White students, it is not significant for the Black or Asian populations. As Allen (1992) suggests, there is a "need for further study of *how* social context affects the academic performance of African American college students" (p.

Table 4.5: Social capital correlates of continued enrollment and graduation, Black students

Predictor Variable	Model 1 Exp(B)	Model 2 Exp(B)	Model 3 Exp(B)	Model 4a Exp(B)	Model 4b Exp(B)
Background characteristics					
Immigrant or second-generation	0.957	0.790	0.761	0.773	0.761
Native	ref	ref	ref	ref	ref
Female	0.922	0.825	0.857	0.891	0.856
Male	ref	ref	ref	ref	ref
Mother's education	1.201	1.345	1.342	1.298	1.340
Father's education	0.849	0.771	0.774	0.779	0.771
Parents' income	1.037	1.034	1.048	1.069	1.055
High school factors					
High school grade point average		3.221 **	3.276 **	3.216 **	3.291 **
SAT I score		1.000	1.000	0.999	1.000
Campus selectivity					
Flagships			0.975	1.099	0.956
Competitive			1.510	1.563	1.481
Less competitive			ref	ref	ref

Table 4.5: Social capital correlates of continued enrollment and graduation, Black students (Continued)

Predictor Variable	Model 1 Exp(B)		Model 2 Exp(B)	Model 3 Exp(B)	Model 4a Exp(B)		Model 4b Exp(B)
Social capital variables							
Interethnic conversations					1.493		
Social integration							1.099
Constant	4.654	***	0.070	0.061	0.035	*	0.058
Number of cases	422		347	347	342		347
Nagelkerke R^2	0.011		0.074	0.083	0.089		0.083

*significant at the 0.05 level, **significant at the 0.01 level, ***significant at the 0.001 level. The notation "ref" is for the reference category of a set of variables.

Table 4.6: Social capital correlates of continued enrollment and graduation, Chicano/Latino students

Predictor Variable	Model 1 Exp(B)	Model 2 Exp(B)	Model 3 Exp(B)	Model 4a Exp(B)	Model 4b Exp(B)
Background characteristics					
Immigrant or second-generation	1.077	1.094	1.069	1.070	1.051
Native	ref	ref	ref	ref	ref
Female	1.211	1.171	1.158	1.150	1.182
Male	ref	ref	ref	ref	ref
Mother's education	1.027	1.009	1.022	1.031	1.016
Father's education	1.056	1.010	1.012	1.007	1.015
Parents' income	1.055	1.031	1.047	1.041	1.039
High school factors					
High school grade point average		3.685 ***	3.156 ***	3.220 ***	3.119 ***
SAT I score		1.000	1.000	1.000	1.000

Table 4.6: Social capital correlates of continued enrollment and graduation, Chicano/Latino students (Continued)

Predictor Variable	Model 1 Exp(B)	Model 2 Exp(B)	Model 3 Exp(B)	Model 4a Exp(B)	Model 4b Exp(B)
Campus selectivity					
Flagships			1.491 *	1.488 *	1.387
Competitive			1.245	1.231	1.206
Less competitive			ref	ref	ref
Social capital variables					
Interethnic conversations				1.212	
Social integration					1.417 **
Constant	3.902 ***	0.022 ***	0.041 ***	0.027 ***	0.034 ***
Number of cases	2763	2187	2187	2166	2179
Nagelkerke R^2	0.005	0.065	0.068	0.070	0.073

*significant at the 0.05 level, **significant at the 0.01 level, ***significant at the 0.001 level. The notation "ref" is for the reference category of a set of variables.

Table 4.7: Social capital correlates of continued enrollment and graduation, Asian students

Predictor Variable	Model 1 Exp(B)		Model 2 Exp(B)		Model 3 Exp(B)		Model 4a Exp(B)		Model 4b Exp(B)	
Background characteristics										
Immigrant or second-generation	0.606	*	0.673		0.657		0.660		0.663	
Native	ref		ref		ref				ref	
Female	1.456	**	1.413	***	1.395	***	1.393	***	1.395	***
Male	ref		ref		ref				ref	
Mother's education	0.963		0.937		0.944		0.937		0.942	
Father's education	1.116	*	1.059		1.056		1.066		1.056	
Parents' income	1.056		1.067		1.086		1.081		1.084	
High school factors										
High school grade point average			3.973	***	3.169	***	3.155	***	3.155	***
SAT I score			1.001	*	1.000		1.000		1.000	

Table 4.7: Social capital correlates of continued enrollment and graduation, Asian students (Continued)

Predictor Variable	Model 1 Exp(B)		Model 2 Exp(B)		Model 3 Exp(B)		Model 4a Exp(B)		Model 4b Exp(B)	
Campus selectivity										
Flagships					1.687	**	1.634	**	1.642	**
Competitive					1.101		1.078		1.085	
Less competitive					ref		ref		ref	
Social capital variables										
Interethnic conversations							1.009			
Social integration									1.104	
Constant	11.904	**	0.025	***	0.075	***	0.072	***	0.074	***
Number of cases	8324		7039		7039		6984		7018	
Nagelkerke R^2	0.012		0.073		0.077		0.075		0.076	

*significant at the 0.05 level, **significant at the 0.01 level, ***significant at the 0.001 level. The notation "ref" is for the reference category of a set of variables.

Table 4.8: Social capital correlates of continued enrollment and graduation, White students

Predictor Variable	Model 1 Exp(B)	Model 2 Exp(B)	Model 3 Exp(B)	Model 4a Exp(B)	Model 4b Exp(B)
Background characteristics					
Immigrant or second-generation	1.109	1.190	1.178	1.192	1.170
Native	ref	ref	ref	ref	ref
Female	1.323 ***	1.163	1.159	1.175	1.161
Male	ref	ref			
Mother's education	0.967	0.985	0.991	0.995	0.988
Father's education	1.182 ***	1.177 **	1.179 **	1.181 **	1.172 **
Parents' income	1.029	1.026	1.027	1.029	1.022
High school factors					
High school grade point average		4.606 ***	3.644 ***	3.639 ***	3.648 ***
SAT 1 score		1.000	1.000	1.000	1.000

Table 4.8: Social capital correlates of continued enrollment and graduation, White students (Continued)

Predictor Variable	Model 1 Exp(B)		Model 2 Exp(B)		Model 3 Exp(B)		Model 4a Exp(B)		Model 4b Exp(B)	
Campus selectivity										
Flagships					1.824	***	1.833	***	1.735	***
Competitive					1.785	***	1.801	***	1.715	***
Less competitive					ref		ref		ref	
Social capital variables										
Interethnic conversations							0.981			
Social integration									1.412	***
Constant	5.784	***	0.011	***	0.025	***	0.024	***	0.021	***
Number of cases	9010		7175		7150		7125		7150	
Nagelkerke R²	0.009		0.072		0.164		0.081		0.086	

*significant at the 0.05 level, **significant at the 0.01 level, ***significant at the 0.001 level. The notation "ref" is for the reference category of a set of variables.

41, emphasis added). Social integration *is* important for these populations (as the qualitative findings on Black students will show), but its relationship to educational outcomes is not straightforward. In addition, there may be other, more salient factors affecting Black student graduation that are obscured when social scientists fail to disaggregate by ethnicity or attempt to fit models that were generated based on White students, to students of other ethnicities.

RESULTS FROM THE QUALITATIVE DATA

I now move to the qualitative data to delve into the characteristics and processes of social capital for Black students at one campus. The University of California campus where I conducted interviews has a strong Black community consisting of an African-American theme dorm, Black pre-professional student groups, Black ethnic groups, student organizations that reach out to Black prospective students, and informal social networks. There are various events coordinated by components of the Black community such as a weekend to recruit admitted students, a weekly gathering where students play games near the main thoroughfare on campus, cultural celebrations, and the organizations' weekly or bimonthly meetings.

Bridging immigrant and native Black students
Interviewees spoke of the Black network on campus as a monolith rather than separate groups of immigrant Blacks and native Blacks. This finding does not match the research that showed social distance that middle-class immigrant Blacks attempt to put between themselves and native Blacks (Waters 1999, Kasinitaz, et al. 2008), but it resonates with Smith and Moore's work (2000). This may be because the present study and that of Smith and Moore (2000) were conducted at colleges. The paucity of Blacks on campus may predispose Black students to join together regardless of immigrant generation. The niche of the Black student community makes the enormity of the campus manageable for this very small group (Nagasawa and Wong 1999).

It can be difficult to meet friends at a college where the classes are large and the students come from diverse backgrounds. Ezinne, a Nigerian American student, explained how the Black community on campus, despite its smallness, filled this void:

I really like the Black people here. [Even] seeing how small our numbers are, it's not like you can go on campus and you say, 'I don't see any Black people.' You'll see Black people. Black people are out, even though we have small numbers, we're out. That's a good thing. (Ezinne, Nigerian American female, second-year student)

Respondents were aware of the small numbers of Black students on campus. They lamented the fact, but also saw it is as a call for Black students to be active members of an ethnic community. Ezinne went on to discuss the closeness of Black students and indicated a lack of division in the community:

As far as the African American slash Black slash from Africa, whatever, they're really, really close and they're really, really supportive as far as the upperclassmen supporting the underclassmen. (Ezinne)

Another Nigerian American student said she feels singled out and isolated when she was the only Black student in a class. She explained:

In class, when I'm the only Black person, you stand out, for one. You represent the Black community. All eyes are on you... You could be the only Black person and people might not want to be in a group with you or people have their other friends in the class and you're just by yourself. Then people form their own groups and you're not in any group. (Ozioma, Nigerian American, first-year student)

Ozioma found herself searching for other Black students in her classes. She gave the example of a class in which there was one other Black person:

If we work in groups, we'll look at each other to form a group. She would be the first person I would try to form a group with. We don't even have to know each other, we just feel comfortable with one another. We have the same background.

We speak alike. I'd just form a group with her, rather than someone else from a different place. (Ozioma)

Ozioma did not differentiate between immigrant and native Black students. "We don't even have to know each other," she said; she was searching her classes for a Black classmate, a fellow member of the Black community.

Interviewees speak of a Black community, inclusive of immigrant and native Black students. Many of the remaining interviews also imply the unity of the Black student network, regardless of family immigration history. Perhaps just as telling, no respondents mentioned social distance between immigrant and native Blacks. Although they articulated differences in culture and academic outlooks (as I described in Chapter 6), they did not mention barriers to bridging these differences and to forming an inclusive Black network.

Typologies of social integration
In terms of ethnicity, Black students may have bonding (co-ethnic) or bridging (inter-ethnic) social capital, or both. From analysis of the interview data, the ethnicity of their three closest friends, and the ethnic base of the student groups to which they belonged, the respondents' tendency to one of the three typologies emerged. I present their narratives about why they chose their path of social integration.

My recruitment methods – beginning with ethnic-based student groups then snowball sampling – biased the sample toward students who are socially integrated in the Black community. I sought out interview respondents who were not part of ethnic-based student groups by visiting classes to solicit participants and by asking interviewees for names of potential respondents who were *not* members of these groups. I use my data to generate categories of social integration, and explore the respondents' explanations of how and why they are in bridging or bonding networks, or both.

Despite organizing respondents into these typologies, their movement among the types is commonplace. This fluidity of social integration is evident in some of the quotes. Students are trying out different groups, have desires to explore other networks, or are unhappy with their present community.

Embedded in the Black community

The social circles of several respondents were circumscribed by the Black student network on campus. Eleven of the 39 respondents were embedded in the Black community. The Black students on campus are a closed group; they all know each other, at least by sight. In fact, interviewees expressed surprise and bafflement when seeing Black students whom they did *not* know. A closed social structure can effectively enforce norms (Coleman 1988). Although it was not a specific question in the interview, several respondents (6 of 39) mentioned feeling pressure to stay within the Black student community. Previous studies on Black college students showed that there is a strong norm of socializing with only co-ethnics (Willie 2003, Smith and Moore 2000, Harper and Quaye 2007). When viewed in this way, social capital can be restrictive (Portes 1998). Thus, the network bonding Black students together could also serve to restrict the development of bridging social capital. The first part of this section explains the sense of obligation that Black students have to participate in the Black community on campus. My findings are similar to those of Willie (2003) who used retrospective interviews with African American alumni of Northwestern University who attended in the post-Civil Rights era. Willie (2003: loc 744) found that "participating in and shoring up the boundaries of a subordinate racial community felt compulsory for many students."

Kiara, a native Black student, explained, "At [her university], since there are not a lot of us, it's always up to a certain few to lead the community or to project who we should be." She wondered about Black students who are not part of the Black community:

> There are those Black people where it's like they're not Black at all. You don't see them with anyone Black. You don't see them at any Black events. You don't have anything to tie them to. They're pretty much not accounted for. No one knows them. (Kiara, native Black female, fourth-year student)

To her, these students are "not Black at all." So, to be a Black student is to be friends with co-ethnics on campus and to participate in ethnic organizations. In her study, Willie (2003:loc 727) found that "black students who socialized with whites were not considered members of the in-group."

Some Black students reacted to their underrepresentation on campus by actively participating in Black student groups and consciously staying within their social circle of Black friends. They believe they are increasing the strength and visibility of the Black community. Jahzara a young native Black woman explained the importance of an active Black student community:

> We have to fight for so much with this university and the bureaucracy and the cutting of student groups. Things that, on a larger spectrum, might not be that important as far as what's going on in the world, but you need to build that community on campus because it's so, so, so, so important to retention of Black folks. (Jahzara, native Black female, third-year student)

She belonged to three Black or minority student groups and all three of her closest friends were Black. Her favorite thing about college was the feeling of support and community that she felt with her friends. Perhaps because of her experience being welcomed to campus by a strong Black community, Jahzara believed that Black students have an obligation to the Black community. They need to join and lead the Black organizations, especially those that recruit and retain Black students on campus.

Jahzara was surprised when she encountered Black students who didn't feel the same obligation to the Black student community:

> I meet people who aren't involved in any student groups. It baffles me. As a Black student, it's kind of your job. A lot of Black students are spread thin because they have to do so much work because there's not that many of us to do the work. (Jahzara)

Upon entering the university, Black students have a ready-made social world consisting of the Black student network. Programs such as the African-American theme dorm and Black student groups make it easy for students to stay within the Black community. A young Black woman who said that her favorite aspect of college was taking classes about African American culture, discussed her social sphere in college:

> Ever since the beginning I've always had this vision, I gotta' hang out with the Black people... then I found the African American Theme Program [residential program for Black students] and I would rather be here with all these Black people that I met at this organization... since I already knew these people, I was like, 'Well, let me go to the African American Theme Program.' So, that's what I did. (Raven, native Black female, first-year student)

Her pool of potential friends was from the African-American dorm and the Black student groups that are promoted there. At the time of the interview, she was in the second half of her first year in college.

Raven talked about the possibility of making friends with students of different ethnicities, but didn't seem proactive about seeking such friends:

> I live... on two floors of Black people... I haven't really started to venture out that much, but I have possibly four more years here. The only thing that's being offered to us really club-wise is things that are organized by Black people. (Raven)

Black students are underrepresented on campus and some feel an obligation to this small community. Participating in Black student groups is a way to increase the presence of Black students and to make the community stronger. Adenike, a Nigerian American student, discussed the need to speak up for the Black community, "I feel like Black people have to represent for the entire race because there are no Black people in the UC system, especially Black men." She was open to friendships with students of other ethnicities, but felt an obligation to the Black community:

> I don't mind branching out [meeting students of other races] but it's not one of my priorities, especially because the [Black]

community is so small here.   I want to help us grow.
(Adenike, U.S.-born Nigerian American, first-year student)

She did not see herself taking pains to befriend students of other ethnicities.   She had leadership roles in the two Black student organizations to which she belonged and saw her participation in those groups growing.

She further explained her unwillingness to branch out:
It's not that I want to segregate myself from anybody, but I feel like people are naturally drawn to where they feel comfortable, where they don't have to explain things as much. (Adenike)

As some respondents have already mentioned, Adenike felt emotionally supported in the Black network.

Alexis, a native Black student, could not participate frequently in student groups because of commitments at work and school, but said she felt pressured to stay involved just enough so that she was still part of the Black student community.   She belonged to three Black or minority student groups.   She discussed her struggle to branch out:

Sometimes it feels a little weird because I think people of the Black community expect me to hang out with, really hang out with, just people of the Black community.   And that's weird. Sometimes I feel the pressure to stay with them, but because I know who I am and I'm secure within myself, I don't care to stay just with them. (Alexis, native Black female, second-year student)

She disclosed that she had just started dating a White student and worried that her Black friends or acquaintances would not approve:

I'm dating and involved with a White guy, but I'm reluctant to tell everyone in the community because, you know?   I don't know, I'm just reluctant.   I don't want to deal with some of the backlash, because there's gonna be someone or a small group of people who are gonna question my Blackness and all of that. (Alexis)

Unlike other respondents already mentioned, this young Black woman did not feel supported by her social network of fellow Black students. She felt pressured to participate in their student groups and to hide her relationship with a non-Black student.

Black students have also been met with prejudice when venturing out of the Black community. One native Black respondent said the hardest part of college so far was the lowered expectations that people had for her as a Black person. To avoid prejudiced classmates, Sherice said she tended to stay within the Black community.

I don't really talk to [non-Black] students. I'm not in any other diverse group and I feel like they would turn against me. Like in Chemistry lab, I feel like no one wants to be my partner because they think I'm not as smart or I'm not capable or I don't want do the work. (Sherice, native Black female, third-year student)

She worried about one class where the graduate student instructor (GSI) asked the students to find different partners so they could meet new people. She asked the GSI if she could stay with her first partner, a friend who was Black also. Sherice went to great lengths to avoid a situation in which non-Black students could reject her or question her academic ability.

Chika, a Nigerian respondent, explained how she felt excluded when a class was breaking up into groups:

They just spontaneously form groups with you left out. So groups would be here and here, and you have to go and actively seek people, and half the people at the table would have their heads down when you ask them, 'Can I join your group?' (Chika, Nigerian female, second-year student)

Her classmates did not question her academic ability out loud. They didn't voice their reluctance to have her join their group, yet she was "left out" and actively ignored because she is Black. Chika held a

Regent Scholarship at her college, a prestigious award which comes with a financial award and on-campus privileges, such as preferential housing and library access. In her case, the financial portion of the scholarship was generous: tuition, fees, and living expenses. On the day that I interviewed her, she was dressed in formal business clothes because she had an interview for a research position at a hospital later that day. She told me that her classmates in math and science classes eventually got to know her:

> I'm taking a genetics lab class right now and this is people who have the same major. I've taken like five classes with them, so someone actually asked me, 'Let's be lab partners.' It's different. They know that you're a good student and you actually do the work. (Chika)

In the follow-up questionnaire one year after the interview, Chika indicated that she would be working at the Johns Hopkins Medical Institute.

Respondents who were embedded in the Black network on campus were committed to the community that bonds Black students together. They felt an obligation to participate in their small co-ethnic group, to make it strong. This obligation felt restrictive to some. In the next section, I present cases of respondents who have a foot in the Black student community while simultaneously stepping into ethnically-diverse networks.

Anchored, but branching out
The majority of the respondents (26 of 39) were anchored in the Black community on campus while branching into networks of different ethnic composition. Here my findings diverge from those of Willie (2003) whose respondents described two separate worlds at Northwestern during that time (late 1960s until 1989) – black and white. These students are like those academically successful individuals with bridging and bonding social capital described in the existing literature. Gibson (1988) described Punjabi Sikh immigrants in a U.S. high school accommodating the dominant culture while maintaining their cultural identity. Carter (2005) presented cultural straddlers as one of three types of minority high school students – they

embrace the dominant culture as well as their nondominant culture. Allen (1985) discussed Black college students who are integrated into different facets of the campus community – Black, White, student, faculty.

Black students were able to benefit from the support of the Black community while also forming close relationships with students of other ethnicities. For some, a common interest, such as religion or a sport, brought them into cross-ethnic groups. Others actively seek ethnic diversity in their networks.

During the course of the interview, I asked students about their activity in on-campus groups and about their network of friends at college. Ten of the 39 Black students I interviewed talked about wanting to branch out of the Black community, about making friends with students of different ethnicities, and about joining student groups that did not have many Black students.

First I present Aaliyah, who was in motion between two paths of social integration. She was embedded in the Black community, but yearned to bridge the ethnic divide into other networks. Aaliyah felt that her college experience will be richer for having relationships with students of different ethnicities. She was halfway through her first year in college and felt sequestered in the Black community:

> The Black community [on campus] is pretty strong. I actually feel uncomfortable being in the Black community so much because I'm not used to it, that sort of isolation. I'm used to more diverse settings. I haven't met anyone else here who wasn't Black. I think as I get older here, I'm going to really try to create more open groups, more open activities, events, that more people can come. There's so much more you can get out of [college] than just one community. (Aalyiah, native Black female, first-year student)

The two on-campus groups she belongs to were for Black students. Yet her favorite aspect of college was the diversity of choices, "I like walking down [main entrance] and getting bombarded with a bunch of different things. There are a lot of opportunities." Aaliyah was firmly in the Black community, but she was eager to meet students of other ethnicities and join ethnically diverse student groups.

Bekele, an Ethiopian student, chose not to live in the African-American dorm his first year and he was consciously striving to make friends of different ethnicities. He explained his rationale for living in a mixed-ethnicity dorm:

> I like to see other African Americans and have that community. It's not that I don't like living with all African Americans, I don't like living with one ethnic group at all, like any, if I was with all Asians or all White people or all African Americans, it's the same to me. I don't want to be in one bubble. I like the mixing. (Bekele, U.S.-born Ethiopian male, first-year student)

His favorite thing about college was the diversity of the students, ethnically and in terms of their viewpoints. Bekele did not belong to any ethnic-oriented groups and, while two of his closest friends were Ethiopian, one was Chinese.

Mary, a native Black respondent, was an active member of a Christian group on campus. She felt a strong sense of belonging to that group:

> In the [Christian student group], it's predominantly Asian and I'd say there's maybe ten other people out of 100 or so that are not Asian American. I feel like, I just don't feel like the one Black person in the crowd. I feel like my identity as a Christian is stronger there. When I'm surrounded by people who identify with a certain identity that you do, you feel that identity more strongly. Living on the floor with African Americans, I feel my African American identity stronger. (Mary, native Black female, first-year student)

Although she said her three closest friends are Black, many of the friends she'd made in college were from student groups, "I'd say more of my friends that I've found with the clubs rather than living in the [African-American themed] dorms." (Mary) Mary had high bridging and bonding social capital.

Brandi was also involved in a Christian campus group and described the group as ethnically mixed. When discussing the

Christian group she belonged to, Brandi attributed the small Black representation to the fact that the percent of Blacks in the larger population is small as well. She described the ethnic makeup of the group:

> It's pretty mixed up. I'd say the largest majority is Whites and Asians. I think it's pretty much the American demographic. Black people are a very small population of America. (Brandi, native Black female, first-year student)

She also was interested in joining swimming and crew, two sports that didn't have many Black students. Sports and religion were drawing this respondent into non-Black student groups.

Respondents who were anchored in the network bonding Black students together *and* networks bridging across ethnicities gave two rationales for branching out of the Black community on campus: the explicit desire to befriend students of other ethnicities, and membership in networks that are ethnically diverse, such as religious groups or athletic teams.

Outside the Black community

Two respondents of the 39 are not part of the Black community on campus. To Willie's (2003) Northwestern alumni, Black students who were not part of the Black community were considered "not black." I found the same sentiment in this study's respondents, epitomized by the student who said, "it's like they're not Black at all." Who are these Black students and why aren't they part of the network bonding Black students together? The two I interviewed had different reasons: one left the Black community the other was never part of it.

Shanice was a third-year Black student who participated in two Black campus groups when she first started college, then stopped attending their meetings. She told me,

> Freshman year, I was more around African American students and all of them were super defensive as well. 'Everyone's racist!' They say, "I heard this white guy came up to my friend and said, 'Oh, are you on an athletic scholarship?'" Someone made a mistake and they're going around telling

everyone. People have asked me, 'Are you on an athletic scholarship?' but I didn't take it as seriously as I would have freshman year... I don't care. Even if you think I'm an athlete, I told you I'm not. (Shanice, native Black female, third-year student)

Shanice lived in the African-American theme dorm her freshman year, purposefully branched out after that and now, in her third year in college, she said her three closest friends are Asian.

Growing up and in high school, Shanice's closest friends were Black. Her high school was mostly Black and Latino students. She described the change her second year in college:

I was more interactive with my floor-mates and I was the only Black person... And so I just hung out with them more and I thought less of myself as Black, instead of always thinking about it. (Shanice)

She said that when she was with her three closest friends, who are Korean, Chinese, and Indian, she could be herself and think less about being Black.

Oladapo, a Nigerian American student, said his three closest friends are Asian. When he was interviewed, he was in his fourth year and had graduated at the time of the follow-up survey. Throughout high school, he had many Black friends who went on to community college, four-year colleges, and some on athletic scholarships to college. His family was also actively part of the larger Ngwa community in Los Angeles, so he had many Nigerian American friends.

Throughout college, Oladapo did not belong to any clubs or groups on campus. He claimed, "I wasn't really into the clubs. I was mainly like a loner. I liked to stay in my dorm." He viewed his inter-ethnic friendships as a by-product of the ethnic makeup of the school, which is largely Asian and White. When asked about his friends in college, he said:

My roommates are currently three Asians. They're predominantly Asian, some Whites as well, a few African

Americans. A quite diverse group of people, but primarily Asians. (Oladapo, U.S.-born Nigerian male, fourth-year student)

He had a hard time meeting people when he got to college and his friends were made in class. Although Oladapo has "a few" Black friends on campus, he can hardly be thought of as "anchored" in the Black community. As with Shanice who actively left the Black network on campus, Oladapo found his niche outside of the Black student community.

Benefits of the Black network: social support
It is well established in the literature that integration into the Black community can aid students in their transition to and integration into the school setting (Allen 1992, Tatum 1999, Museus 2008, Murguia, Padilla, and Pavel 1991, Price, Hyle, and Jordan 2009). Although not specifically prompted to speak about it, 15 of the 39 interviewees discussed the social and academic support they received from the Black community on campus.

Some Black students saw ethnic-oriented student groups and the general Black student community as a niche in a huge university. Maurice, a native Black student explained the situation for many Black students when they arrive on campus:

The university is so big and there are so many places that you could possibly fit into that you really have to find a place where you feel comfortable and where people relate to you and where you relate to them and you get along. (Maurice, native Black male, first-year student)

For him, those organizations were a Black business student group and an athletic team.

Maurice spoke of the importance of finding others who would understand his unique experiences as a Black man in America. The example he gave was that students of other ethnicities did not believe that Black men are routinely pulled over for "driving while Black." He also felt a kinship to other Black college students, an understanding that:

When I'm around Black people, I can act stereotypically Black and even though it's not really a part of my personality, it's just part of the atmosphere. Especially if you're at a party, you just get out there and for that moment, while you're dancing, it's ok to be stereotypically Black if you want to, be whitewashed if you want to. Especially here [respondent's college] where there's definitely more Black kids who are academically sound, it's ok also to sometimes be whitewashed... It's ok to focus on your schoolwork and study. (Maurice)

In the Black community at school, Maurice had found peers who relate to him as a Black man and as a serious student. Of all the on-campus networks he could have joined, he found the embrace of the Black community comfortable and reassuring.

In many ways, the benefits of the Black student community are offered by other on-campus groups also: supportive upperclassmen, a niche in an intimidatingly large university, and information on how to navigate university administration. On the other hand, respondents discuss the additional offerings of the Black network on campus: empathetic support for the unique experiences of Black people, understanding of the multiple identities possible as Blacks, and an easily-identifiable, welcoming community.

Benefits of the Black community: academic support
Another facet of support that the Black community provides is academic. The statistical analysis in the first part of this chapter questions the link between Black students' social integration and their academic success; however, at this campus, I found that many respondents relied upon the informal Black student network as well as organized Black and minority student groups for academic assistance.

Entering large, introductory classes, underclassmen may feel uncomfortable and seek the company of other Black students for mutual support, as already mentioned in the previous section. Students described looking for other Black students when entering a class or a lab at the beginning of the semester. They were searching for a friendly classmate to sit next to, a study group, a lab partner.

Imani, a native Black student, described a large, introductory class in Political Science:

> There's about ten Black people, I believe they're all girls too. I sit by five of them, the other five or four are freshmen and they sit together. There's 300 people in the class, in [a large lecture hall]. (Imani, native Black female, second-year student)

She went on to explain how at the beginning of the semester, Black students look for each other and decide as a group where they will sit in the lecture hall. The Black student network bonds students together, making the intimidating size of a lecture hall manageable.

Many Black students who are science majors find academic support through minority programs specifically for science students. Robel, an Eritrean student talked about his experience:

> Just being a minority, that makes it difficult, especially in the sciences, it's even lower representation of minorities. It just makes it difficult especially when you're first coming in, the transition period, that was the hardest for me, not seeing people who look like you... It's just, still, you're not comfortable. You're trying to figure out things on your own. You don't feel like you have... even if you do have avenues to get help, you feel like you don't have them because you don't feel like you can relate to those people who may be trying to help you. (Robel, Eritrean male who immigrated to the U.S. at age two, fourth-year student)

He struggled in his classes and found:

> The first couple years I was always on my own. I was always in the library on my own, studying on my own. I didn't really study with anybody... By my second year, I joined [support group for minority science students]... As soon as I was in [the support group], I would always be in that room studying with other people. I could see the difference. (Robel)

At the time of the interview, Robel was a fourth-year student who aspired to a joint MD/PhD degree. In the follow-up questionnaire, one year after the interview, he had graduated from college and was applying to graduate programs.

DISCUSSION

The concept of social capital is useful for examining the way the Black student experience differs from the experiences of students of other ethnicities. The factors affecting social integration and bridging social capital differ for Black students as compared with other students. In the models with all UC students (Table 4.1), gender, college grade point average, and immigrant generation were significant predictors of whether students were socially integrated. These factors were not significantly related to the social integration of Black students (Table 4.2). Similarly, the significant predictors of bridging social capital for all UC students (Table 4.3) were gender, socioeconomic status, and high school academic performance. These findings differ from the model with only Black students (Chapter 3, Table 3.5) in which only SAT I score is related to bridging social capital.

The predominant model of student attrition (Tinto 1993) predicts that social integration will have a positive effect on graduation. I found evidence for this relationship in statistical models for all UC students (Table 4.4), White students (Table 4.8), and Chicano/Latino students (Table 4.6). Some empirical research suggests that social integration and graduation are linked for minority students (Murguia, Padilla, and Pavel 1991), but studies specifically on Black students have not found this relationship significant (Mallinckrodt 1988, Allen 1992). In the statistical analyses of present study, Black students' social integration was not related to their graduation.

These quantitative results call for theories of college educational performance that take into account the unique processes of social integration experienced by students of different ethnicities. There is a need for researchers to deeply explore how and why Black students integrate into the social life of their college campuses. Some research on Black college student social integration attempts to fit models created for White students onto this unique population (Tinto 1993). Other researchers critique these attempts (Museus and Maramba 2011,

Allen 1992, Tierney 1999). Promising models of academic performance fitted specifically for Black students emphasize cultural integrity and cultural flexibility (Carter 2010, Tierney 1999).

Although the statistical analysis did not show a significant relationship between Black students' social integration and graduation, the interview data highlights the role of the Black student community in providing academic assistance. Respondents discussed the academic support they received and the social connections they made that helped them adapt to and succeed in college. In these ways, bonding social capital helps Black students. There are several possible explanations for the apparent disconnect between the statistical findings and the interview data. Although Black respondents talked about the support of student groups, membership in these networks may have been a social benefit rather than an academic benefit. The discrepancy may also be reconciled in light of Nagasawa and Wong's (1999) theory of minority student success: that ethnic niches are necessary, but not sufficient components of minority student survival in college. Another explanation is suggested by Tinto (1993): while advocating policies that would place ethnic-based student groups in the mainstream of campus life, Tinto suggests that ethnic groups are most often found on the periphery. Thus, the academic benefits of social integration into these groups are dampened.

The qualitative analysis also revealed that respondents speak of the Black community in terms of immigrant and native students together. This unity across immigrant generations joins with a similar finding by Smith and Moore (2000) in questioning the division between immigrant and native Blacks (Waters 1999, Vickermann 1999, Kasinitz, et al. 2008), at least in certain circumstances. I attribute the lack of social distance between these two groups within the Black community to the environment specific to the university. The paucity of Black students may encourage them to band together, regardless of their family immigration history. There is not much room for differentiation among the Black students since their numbers are so small. Willie (2003:loc 1698) commented, "Black students who are small in number or proportion on a campus are usually aware of one another's personal lives, frustrated that they are so dependent on one another, and cognizant of their differences from one another." She found that Black students at Northwestern formed one, closed community. This resonates with my findings at the interview site.

Interview respondents described their paths of social integration into college. The Black student community played a role for almost all of them. Some were embedded in the Black community. Interviewees talked about the importance of committing time and energy to Black organizations. They reasoned that it was each Black student's obligation to be actively involved in the Black student groups because there were so few Black students. This obligation weighed heavy on some respondents, calling to mind the restrictive nature of bonding social capital (Portes 1998). A few interviewees found themselves, by virtue of their interests, in primarily non-Black student organizations. Other respondents made a conscious effort to branch out of the Black community, to purposefully make friends with students of different ethnicities. Most Black students were already anchored in the Black community when they branched out. Of the 39 respondents, 30 reported that at least two of their three closest friends were Black. A small number of interviewees described their social network as outside of the Black student community. Their reasons for their primarily non-Black social integration differed, but the way they are viewed by other Blacks on campus is the same. Respondents in this study were suspicious of Black students who were not part of the co-ethnic network; this echoes findings from Willie (2003).

CONCLUSION

The vision of the Black student community that emerges from the interviews is one that is cohesive, supportive, and, to some degree, insular. It is common for Black students to be integrated into groups that bond Black students together as well as groups that bridge ethnic differences; however, Black students who are completely outside the Black network are disparaged as "not really Black." These findings, coupled with those in Chapter 3, underscore the idea of a unique Black college experience: immigrant and native Black students belong to the same social network and the social integration of Black students is different from that of their non-Black peers.

Based on the statistical analyses presented in this chapter, Black students need their own model of college attrition, rather an adaptation of a theory generated from data on White students. Black students' experiences and processes are different enough to warrant a re-conceptualization of Tinto's (1993) model of college attrition. Despite the lack of a statistical relationship between Black students' social integration and graduation, the interviews show how important the co-ethnic community is to this population of student. I suggest two complementary explanations: (1) ethnicity-based student groups are most often found on the periphery of campus life, lessening the effect of social integration on retention (Tinto 1993), and (2) social integration may be necessary for most Black students to acclimate to, integrate in, and eventually graduate from college, but it is not enough (Nagasawa and Wong 1999).

CHAPTER 5

Race on Campus

In March 2011, Alexandra Wallace, a White UCLA student posted a video on YouTube.com complaining about the "hordes" of Asian students on campus and mimicking people speaking an Asian language. Her blatant racism was swiftly met with rebukes from the university and college students around the nation (Lovett 2011). It was also a reminder that racism continues to exist on college campuses.

Experiences of discrimination at college

The university is a unique site of discrimination. There is a difference between discrimination in public spaces and discrimination in schools (Kasinitz, et al. 2008). In the former situation, there is little the target of discrimination can do and this leads to anger and discouragement. In the latter situation, the victim can excel in his or her schoolwork to show he or she can succeed. The classroom provides an ongoing forum in which the same students and instructor meet for a period of time. When Black students encounter prejudiced classmates or instructors, they can react by speaking up in class so that they defy lowered expectations. They can perform well on exams to show the instructor that they are capable. The respondents of the present study used these strategies among others.

Prestigious colleges are the training ground for the business, political, and academic leaders of tomorrow. If the university has a hostile racial climate and minority students do not have a strong sense of belonging, then this negatively affects the diversity of the next generation of leaders. Highly educated African Americans are more likely to encounter Whites, and this may account for their higher likelihood of perceiving discrimination as compared with less educated African Americans (Kasinitz, et al. 2008). Students, especially at elite universities such as the one where the present study was conducted, are

133

upwardly mobile and part of a politically active community. Thus, they are exposed to and perhaps particularly attuned to prejudice. Various studies document the discrimination Black students experience in higher education (for example Pewewardy and Frey 2002, Davis, et al. 2004, Price, Hyle, and Jordan 2009). The present study adds to this literature with the additional dimension of family immigration history.

Perceiving discrimination: differences by immigrant generation

Of all the immigrants coming into the United States over the past 50 years, Black immigrants from Africa, the Caribbean, and Latin America are most likely to be conflated with native Blacks in the minds of Americans (Kasinitz, et al. 2008). Thus, immigrant Blacks are exposed to the same interpersonal and institutional racism as native Blacks. Ambiguous encounters with non-Blacks can leave native and immigrant Blacks wondering if they are targets of prejudice or of discriminatory treatment. Within the confines of this study, the question that can be addressed is: Are immigrant Black students less likely than native Black students to perceive discrimination?

John Ogbu's (1991, Ogbu and Simon 1998) theory of voluntary immigrants and involuntary minorities is a relevant lens through which to view the way immigrant Blacks and native Blacks perceive discrimination. Voluntary immigrants, such as Black immigrants and their children, have experienced or heard about life in the sending country. For those from Nigeria and Ethiopia, the United States offers a more open opportunity structure. According to Ogbu, when voluntary immigrants encounter discrimination, they view it as an obstacle to overcome. On the other hand, involuntary minorities, such as native Blacks, have experienced or heard about pervasive institutional racism in the United States. They view discrimination as continual and unrelenting. Thus, immigrant Blacks may be more likely than native Blacks to dismiss ambiguously discriminatory treatment as benign.

Empirical work comparing native and immigrant Blacks' perceptions of discrimination supports Ogbu's theory. In a comparison of native African Americans and West Indian immigrants, Mary Waters (1999) found that West Indian immigrants were less likely to interpret their interactions with White Americans as racialized. In the present study, I extend Ogbu's theory to immigrant *and* second-generation immigrant Blacks and compare their perceptions of discrimination with native Blacks'. Waters did not find the same immigrant optimism among second-generation West Indian immigrants, especially those in racially-segregated, poor neighborhoods. Subsequent research has shown that children of West Indian immigrants experience discrimination as frequently as native Blacks (Kasinitz, et al. 2008).

Discrimination and academic outcomes

When students believe there are prejudiced students, faculty, or staff at their school, it can have an adverse effect on their academic performance and outcomes. African American students who perceive ethnic injustice may devalue academic success (Schmader, Major, and Gramzow 2001, Wong, Eccles, and Sameroff 2003). The stress of a hostile racial climate on campus can have deleterious effects on minorities' college grades (Nadler and Clark 2011, Smedley, Myers, and Harrell 1993). When students perceive negative stereotypes about their group in an academic setting, the threat to their identity as students negatively affects their academic performance (Steele and Aronson 1995). In terms of graduation rates, ethnic minorities have less commitment to an institution when they encounter discrimination (Harper and Hurtado 2007, Cabrera, et al. 1999). Institutional commitment is often used as a proxy for college persistence and graduation (Bean 1985, Gerdes and Mallinckrodt 1994, Cabrera, et al. 1999, Smedley, Myers, and Harrell 1993).

One study challenges the idea that perceived racial injustice is detrimental to academic outcomes. Levin, Van Laar, and Foote (2006) asserted that African Americans who perceive more discrimination have a stronger motivation to get a high GPA. However, the relationship was found non-significant. I test this relationship with the quantitative data.

Perceptions of discrimination: Findings from the statistical data

In this section, I present the regression models across various samples – the full UC population, the campus where the interviews were conducted, Black students across all UC campuses, and Black students at the campus where the interviews were conducted. The dependent variable is a binary categorical variable and the predictor variables are categorical, so I used binary logistic regression to estimate the coefficients. Each variable's odds ratio [Exp(B)] is presented in the tables.

The variable under investigation is a prompt with six closed-ended answers. Respondents chose from a Likert scale ranging from "Strongly Disagree" to "Strongly Agree" to the following statement: Students are respected here regardless of their race or ethnicity. An examination of students' answers by ethnicity is presented in Chapter 3 (Figure 3.1). To summarize, the bivariate relationship suggests that Black students are uniquely attuned to and/or disproportionately victimized by racial discrimination. For the present analysis, the values were dichotomized; one value encompasses "Strongly Disagree" to "Somewhat Agree" and the other value is "Agree" and Strongly Agree." The cut between "Somewhat Agree" and "Agree" captures those respondents who do not feel there is *any* problem with racial discrimination at their school, and compares them to respondents who have some reservations about the racial climate on campus.

Independent variables in the regression models account for ethnicity, immigrant generation, socioeconomic status, and campus. For the full UCUES sample (Table 5.1), the first model has only the dummy variables for ethnicity. For the second model, I added immigrant generation and the measures of socioeconomic status. The third model includes college performance and campus category as correlates. The relationship between college grade point average and whether students believe they are respected may not be unidirectional. If a student believes she is in a respectful and tolerant environment, she may perform better academically. Doing well academically can also lead a student to view her environment as welcoming and pleasant. Thus, for the college performance variable, the relationship to the "dependent variable" is a correlation rather than an assumption of causation. A discussion on how campuses were categorized is found in the Methods chapter of this work. In the last model, interaction terms between ethnicity and immigrant generation are added. Similar sets of models were run on each subsample (Tables 5.2 through 5.4).

According to the regression analyses with the full UCUES sample (Table 5.1), ethnicity is an important predictor of whether a respondent believed that students are respected on campus regardless of race. As I discussed previously, the dependent variable is a measure of discrimination. Asian, Chicano/Latino, and Black students were significantly more likely than White students to perceive their college environment as a site of discrimination. White students were five times more likely than Black students to believe that students are respected regardless of race. White students' likelihood was also significantly greater than that of Asian and Chicano/Latino students, but the magnitude of difference was not as large as for Black students. As the odds ratio approaches 1, the difference in perceiving discrimination, vis-à-vis Whites, is less. The magnitude of the coefficient for Black students may be attributed to their very small representation on campuses and the depth and breadth of racism that has uniquely affected Blacks in the United States.

Immigrant and second-generation immigrant students as compared to native students also perceive more discrimination on campus. Native minorities are less different from the mainstream, perhaps eliciting less discriminatory treatment. Parents' income has a positive effect on whether respondents believe students are respected on campus regardless of race. This measure of family socioeconomic status shows that students who come from more well-off families feel less racial tension on campus. The campuses that are the least academically selective appear to have more comfortable racial environments for students. Students at these campuses, the reference group in the regression models, are more likely to agree that students feel respected at their campus. This finding is consistent for the subpopulation of Black students also (Table 5.3). It may be that selectively is affecting perceptions of discrimination directly or that the campus categories are capturing a different factor such as racial make up or support programs common to the campuses that are grouped together. The important point is that institutional milieu plays a crucial role in minority students' sensitivity to and perceptions of discrimination.

The addition of interaction terms between ethnicity and immigrant or second-generation immigrant status shows that immigrant Chicano/Latino students are more likely to perceive discrimination than native Whites. The Black and Asian interaction terms are not significant. This suggests that Black students, regardless of family immigration history, are similar in their perceptions of discrimination on campus.

Table 5.2 shows the binary logistic regression models for UCUES respondents at the interview site. The UCUES respondents are different from this study's interview respondents. The UCUES data is from Spring term 2004 while the interviews for this study took place during the 2007-08 academic year. I present this UCUES subsample as a general representation of the interview site rather than an exact match for the interview respondents. The interview site, one of the flagship campuses, has large Asian and White representation, but very poor Black representation (see Methods chapter for a detailed analysis of ethnic representation).

As with the models based on students from all UC campuses, Black students at the interview site were much more likely than White students to perceive discrimination (Table 5.2, Model 4). This was true of Asian and immigrant Chicano/Latino students at this campus also.

Table 5.3 presents the regression results for Black students across the UC campuses. Sex is a significant factor in whether or not Black UC students perceive discrimination. The odds of Black women agreeing that students are respected regardless of race are only 0.6 times those of Black men in this model (Table 3, Model 3). As with the previous models on different populations (all UC campuses, Black students at all campuses), there is no difference in perceiving discrimination for immigrant versus native Blacks. This finding is also consistent with other empirical studies (Kasinitz, et al. 2008, Deaux 2006). The large and significant factor affecting perceived discrimination among Black students is the institution. Although the campuses are grouped by selectivity, other institutional factors that are correlated with selectivity may be affecting the relationship. In Chapter 3, a similar analysis of the predictors of perceived discrimination showed a relationship to campus diversity (Table 3.1). At those campuses with high levels of Blacks or underrepresented minorities, Black students were more likely to feel that students were respected.

Ethnicity and campus were significant predictors of perceiving discrimination in the previous models (Table 5.1). Looking specifically at one ethnicity (Black) at one campus (interview site), Table 5.4 shows the regression predicting perceiving discrimination. The first model has only sex and immigrant generation. In this reduced model, immigrant and second-generation immigrant Blacks are 2.5 times more likely than native Blacks to say that students are respected on campus regardless of race or ethnicity. That is, immigrant Blacks are less likely to perceive discrimination on campus. However, once socioeconomic status is taken into account, the immigrant effect is no longer significant.

Table 5.1: Binary logistic regression predicting respondents' belief that students are respected on campus regardless of race

Predictor Variable	Model 1		Model 2		Model 3		Model 4	
	Exp(B)		Exp(B)		Exp(B)		Exp(B)	
Ethnicity								
Black	0.211	***	0.196	***	0.188	***	0.163	***
Chicano/Latino	0.552	***	0.601	***	0.591	***	0.723	***
Asian	0.684	***	0.788	***	0.793	***	0.700	***
White	ref		ref		ref		ref	
Family characteristics								
Immigrant or second-generation			0.853	***	0.853	***	0.885	*
Native			ref		ref		ref	
Female			0.976		0.973		0.974	
Male			ref		ref		ref	
Mother's education			0.991		0.992		0.991	
Father's education			1.000		0.996		0.992	
Income			1.041		1.041	**	1.042	**
College								
UC grade point average					1.076		1.076	*
Flagship campuses					0.756	***	0.757	***

Table 5.1: Binary logistic regression predicting respondents' belief that students are respected on campus regardless of race (Continued)

Predictor Variable	Model 1		Model 2		Model 3		Model 4	
	Exp(B)		Exp(B)		Exp(B)		Exp(B)	
Competitive campuses					0.715	***	0.715	***
Less competitive campuses					ref		ref	
Interaction terms								
Black*Immigrant or second							1.547	
Chicano/Latino* Immigrant or							0.726	**
Asian* Immigrant or second							1.109	
Constant	1.569	***	1.460	***	1.524	***	1.525	***
Number of cases	37,858		20,798		20,798		20,798	
Pseudo R^2 (Nagelkerke)	0.028		0.030		0.035		0.036	

*significant at the 0.05 level, **significant at the 0.01 level, ***significant at the 0.001 level

Table 5.2: Binary logistic regression predicting respondents' belief that students are respected on campus regardless of race, interview site

Predictor Variable	Model 1		Model 2		Model 3		Model 4	
	Exp(B)		Exp(B)		Exp(B)		Exp(B)	
Ethnicity								
Black	0.176	***	0.141	***	0.138	***	0.098	***
Chicano/Latino	0.493	***	0.457	***	0.453	***	0.688	
Asian	0.847	**	0.880		0.878		0.625	*
White	ref		ref		ref		ref	
Family characteristics								
Immigrant or second-generation			1.008		1.008		1.010	
Native			ref		ref		ref	
Female			1.040		1.042		1.045	
Male			ref		ref		ref	
Mother's education			1.003		1.005		1.005	
Father's education			0.958		0.960		0.954	
Income			1.029		1.030		1.032	

Table 5.2: Binary logistic regression predicting respondents' belief that students are respected on campus regardless of race, interview site (Continued)

Predictor Variable	Model 1		Model 2		Model 3		Model 4	
	Exp(B)		Exp(B)		Exp(B)		Exp(B)	
College								
UC grade point average					0.954		0.953	
Interaction terms								
Black*Immigrant or second generation							3.128	
Chicano/Latino* Immigrant or second							0.573	*
Asian* Immigrant or second generation							1.421	
Constant	1.476	***	1.415	**	1.635	*	1.663	*
Number of cases	6928		4386		4386		4386	
Pseudo R² (Nagelkerke)	0.032		0.032		0.032		0.036	

*significant at the 0.05 level, **significant at the 0.01 level, ***significant at the 0.001 level

Table 5.3: Binary logistic regression predicting respondents' belief that students are respected on campus regardless of race, Black students

Predictor Variable	Model 1		Model 2		Model 3	
	Exp(B)		Exp(B)		Exp(B)	
Family characteristics						
Immigrant or second-generation	1.242		1.236		1.313	
Native	ref		ref		ref	
Female	0.526	***	0.600	*	0.598	*
Male			ref		ref	
Mother's education			0.970		0.989	
Father's education			1.055		1.074	
Income			1.189		1.138	
College						
UC grade point average					1.376	
Flagship campuses					0.279	***
Competitive campuses					0.231	***
Less competitive campuses					ref	
Constant	0.505	***	0.233	***	0.214	*
Number of cases	867		439		439	
Pseudo R² (Nagelkerke)	0.029	0.033			0.137	

*significant at the 0.05 level, **significant at the 0.01 level, ***significant at the 0.001 level

The notation "ref" is for the reference category of a set of variables. The dependent variable is responses to "Students are respected here regardless of their race or ethnicity."

Table 5.4: Binary logistic regression predicting respondents' belief that students are respected on campus regardless of race, Black students at interview site

Predictor Variable	Model 1		Model 2		Model 3	
	Exp(B)		Exp(B)		Exp(B)	
Family characteristics						
Immigrant or second-generation	2.483	*	2.593		2.163	
Native	ref		ref		ref	
Female	0.343	**	0.279	**	0.250	**
Male			ref		ref	
Mother's education			--		--	
Father's education			1.071		1.043	
Income			--		--	
College						
UC grade point average					2.858	*
Constant	0.395	**	0.358		0.017	*
Number of cases	182		120		120	
Pseudo R^2 (Nagelkerke)	0.104		0.147		0.197	

*significant at the 0.05 level, **significant at the 0.01 level, ***significant at the 0.001 level
The notation "ref" is for the reference category of a set of variables. The dependent variable is responses to "Students are respected here regardless of their race or ethnicity."

In the previous samples, socioeconomic status was measured with three variables: mother's education, father's education, and student-reported household income. In the sample of Black students at the interview site, using all three socioeconomic status measures reduces the number of cases to below 100. Since differences in father's education are more pronounced than differences in mother's education (see Educational Attainment chapter), father's education was retained in the model. Using only mother's education to represent socioeconomic status would have resulted in more cases (n = 154) for the analysis, but it would have changed the findings.

Effects of discrimination on college grade point average
As shown in the previous regressions on perceptions of discrimination, there is a significant relationship between perceiving discrimination and academic performance. The causal mechanism of this relationship is likely circular. That is, high academic performance and viewing the racial climate as innocuous may reinforce each other. In the following models, perception of discrimination is treated as an independent variable predicting college grade point average or graduation.

For all UC students, believing students are respected regardless of race is not significantly related with UC GPA. I tested this relationship on the subpopulations and found that it was not significant. Perceiving discrimination did not have a significant effect on college grade point average for Black students. This is consistent with a study by Cabrera, et al. (1999) that found that perceiving discrimination on campus is not related to college GPA. Therefore, only the model for all UC students is presented.

Table 5.5 shows the results of the linear regression predicting UC GPA for the full UCUES population. The models take into account background, high school, and campus factors. High school academic performance is highly correlated with college grade point average and graduation. However, I include it in the regression models in order to isolate institutional effects of the university. For example, it seems surprising that increasing campus selectivity decreases UC GPA. The bivariate relationship is positive, but becomes negative when high school grade point average is in the model. This shows that, for students with equal pre-college academic performance, attending a less competitive school results in a higher college grade point average. Consider the student who had a B-average in high school – he is likely

to do better at a less selective college where presumably the coursework is not as challenging.

With these variables taken into account, feeling students are respected on campus is not a significant predictor of college GPA (Table 5.5, Model 4). The non-significance of the discrimination variable is explained by the wording of the original question. Students who took the survey responded to this prompt, "Students are respected here regardless of their race or ethnicity."

Effects of discrimination on graduation
In addition to college grade point average, I tested the relationship of perceiving discrimination on graduation. The relationship between perceiving discrimination and graduation is not significant in any of the subpopulations: interview site, Black students, or Black students at the interview site. This is similar to the study by Cabrera and colleagues (1999) that shows that Black students perceiving discrimination on campus is not significantly related to their persistence. Therefore, the binary logistic regression model I present is only for the full UCUES population (Table 5.6).

The addition of high school factors results in a decrease in the magnitude and significant of the coefficient for Black ethnicity. That is, high school grades and SAT I score go a long way toward explaining the difference in college persistence between Black and White students. Chicano/Latino students are less likely to graduate than White students; while Asian students are more likely to persist. High school performance is a significant predictor of college graduation. There is also a difference in graduate rates by campus selectivity. Students at flagship colleges are 1.7 times more likely to graduate than students at less competitive schools (Table 5.6, Model 3). With these variables taken into account, perceiving discrimination is not significantly related to college graduation.

On the question of differences between immigrant and native Black students, the models based on subpopulations of Black students across the campuses and at the interview site (Tables 5.3 and 5.4) show that the relationship between immigrant generation and perceptions of discrimination are not significant when background factors are taken into account. In addition, models with ethnicity and immigrant status

Table 5.5: Standardized coefficients in linear regression predicting college grade point average, all UC students

Predictor Variable	Model 1 Beta		Model 2 Beta		Model 3 Beta		Model 4 Beta	
Background characteristics								
Black	-0.090	***	-0.032	***	-0.034	***	-0.035	***
Chicano/Latino	-0.129	***	-0.066	***	-0.068	***	-0.069	***
Asian	-0.086	***	-0.108	***	-0.109	***	-0.111	***
White	ref		ref		ref		ref	
Immigrant or second-generation	-0.009		-0.003		-0.003		-0.002	
Native	ref		ref		ref		ref	
Female	0.080	***	0.100	***	0.102	***	0.102	***
Male	ref		ref		ref		ref	
Mother's education	0.046	***	0.012		0.011		0.009	
Father's education	0.133	***	0.041	***	0.032	**	0.033	**
Income	0.028	***	0.025	**	0.024	**	0.024	**
High school factors								
GPA			0.294	***	0.335	***	0.336	***
SAT I score			0.259	***	0.284	***	0.286	***

Table 5.5: Standardized coefficients in linear regression predicting college grade point average, all UC students (Continued)

Predictor Variable	Model 1		Model 2		Model 3		Model 4	
	Beta		Beta		Beta		Beta	
Campus selectivity								
Flagship campuses					-0.144	***	-0.146	***
Competitive campuses					-0.172	***	-0.174	***
Less competitive campuses					ref		ref	
Discrimination								
Feeling respected on campus							-0.011	
Number of cases	20,985		16,875		16,875		16,727	
Adjusted R^2	0.081		0.274		0.286		0.287	

*significant at the 0.05 level, **significant at the 0.01 level, ***significant at the 0.001 level

Table 5.6: Discrimination correlates of graduation or continuing enrollment, all UC students

Predictor Variable	Model 1 Exp(B)		Model 2 Exp(B)		Model 3 Exp(B)		Model 4a Exp(B)	
Background								
Immigrant or second-Native	1.012		1.057		1.036		1.034	
Native	ref		ref		ref		ref	
Female	1.328	***	1.238	***	1.228	***	1.229	***
Male	ref		ref		ref		ref	
Black	0.456	***	0.697	*	0.664	**	0.670	*
Chicano/Latino	0.620	***	0.760	**	0.746	**	0.739	**
Asian	1.211	*	1.226	*	1.224	*	1.220	*
White	ref		ref		ref		ref	
Mother's education	0.990		0.984		0.992		0.994	
Father's education	1.110	***	1.069	*	1.074	*	1.072	*
Parents' income	1.045		1.043		1.056		1.052	
High school factors								
High school grade point			4.109	***	3.346	***	3.329	***
SAT I score			1.000	*	1.000		1.000	

Table 5.6: Discrimination correlates of graduation or continuing enrollment, all UC students (Continued)

Predictor Variable	Model 1 Exp(B)		Model 2 Exp(B)		Model 3 Exp(B)		Model 4a Exp(B)	
Campus selectivity								
Flagships					1.690	***	1.688	***
Competitive					1.394	***	1.397	***
Less competitive					ref		ref	
Discrimination variable								
Feeling respected on							0.997	
Constant	5.253	***	0.017	***	0.039	***	0.040	***
Number of cases	20,519		16,748		16,748		16,600	
Nagelkerke R²	0.024		0.084		0.088		0.087	

*significant at the 0.05 level, **significant at the 0.01 level, ***significant at the 0.001 level

interaction terms (Tables 5.1 and 5.2) do not indicate any difference in Black students' perceptions of discrimination by immigrant generation. The one model based on Black students that showed an immigrant effect on perceiving discrimination (Table 5.4, Model 1) changed when father's education was added (Table 5.4, Model 2). Thus, the immigrant effect is really caused by differential levels of paternal education, with immigrant Black students being more likely to have fathers with advanced degrees. This suggests that, at least in terms of perceiving discrimination, there is a common *Black student experience* within the UC system and at the interview site.

The quantitative data clearly show the unique racial experience of Black students at UC campuses and also at the interview site. They are set apart from students of other ethnicities in terms of feeling (dis)respected because of their race or ethnicity. This was suggested in Chapter 3, where I showed a significant difference in the Black students' versus non-Black students' perceptions of racial discrimination on campus (Figure 3.1). In the present chapter, I use regression models to control for other explanatory variables (immigrant generation, gender, socioeconomic status, college academic performance, and campus selectivity) and still found that Black students were much more likely to perceive discrimination. These findings contribute to the thesis of a *unique Black student experience*, that Black students experience the institution of college differently than non-Black students.

The findings do not suggest a direct relationship between discrimination and academic performance or outcomes. Models testing the effect of perceiving discrimination on college grade point average (Table 5.5) and on graduation (Table 5.6) did not yield significant results. In addition, the bivariate relationships between perceiving discrimination and educational outcomes (college grade point average or graduation) were not significant for any population: all UC students, Black UC students, students at the interview site, or Black students at the interview site. Scholarly work in this area suggests that there is a negative relationship between discrimination and persistence in college (Harper and Hurtado 2007, Cabrera, et al. 1999). The findings in this chapter do not definitively support the extant empirical studies. As I discuss in the next section, the interview data offer some explanation for the lack of a statistical relationship between discrimination and academic performance.

FINDINGS FROM THE INTERVIEW DATA

Experiences of discrimination in college
The university is a unique site of discrimination. Before matriculating, Black students might expect very little racial prejudice in this egalitarian environment filled with educated instructors and open-minded peers. However, the quantitative analysis has shown that Black UC students encounter racial discrimination at higher rates than do students of other ethnicities (Table 5.1). Instances of racial discrimination on campus were recounted by most interviewees (21 of 39).

Interviewees attribute experiences of discrimination to non-Black classmates, particularly White and Asian students, who are from neighborhoods and schools where there are few or no Blacks. This may result in stereotypical images of Blacks based on media portrayals.

Kim, a native Black student, talked about how negative stereotypes of Blacks emerge when non-Black students grow up in a sheltered environment:

> A lot of these people grew up in neighborhoods where there were no Black people, so their only representation of my race was what they saw on TV. We all know how lovely Black people are portrayed, minorities in general, are portrayed on television. No, that's not my favorite rapper. No, I don't only listen to rap music. Yes, I can swim. Yes, I've heard of that movie. Yes, I've read that book. Apparently all African Americans are sheltered. I try to show that I'm not just my color. (Kim, native Black female, second-year student)

She understood that students who don't know many Black people might have stereotypical images of Blacks. She felt compelled to prove those stereotypes wrong.

Robert, another native Black student said that non-Black students may have never seen Black people in schools or engaged in academics:

> They [students of other ethnicities] probably look at me different because they're not used to having African American students around. They probably came from private schools

which is majority Caucasian and Asian students and never experienced African American students and how they involve themselves in academic situations other than what they've seen in the media. (Robert, native Black male, first-year student)

He told me that he was careful not to fulfill negative stereotypes that non-Black students might have about Blacks.

For example, let's say I'm late for class. That happens to everybody, right? In the case that you're late for class, what do you want to do? You want to run to class, right? But I feel the need to *not* run to class because I feel like there's an expectation, because I'm African American, and there's a stereotype that African Americans are late for everything. So I don't want to fulfill that stereotype. This is a campus full of everybody and they probably haven't seen that many African Americans because there aren't that many African Americans on campus. When they see me running, so they're like, 'Wait, this is the only African American that *I've* seen and they're just running and late for everything.' I don't want to give that stigma… If I was late, I'd try my best not to run. I'd try to speed walk. [laughs] (Robert)

The feeling among Black college students that they represent their race to others on campus has been documented in the literature (Feagin 1992, Davis, et al. 2004, Price, Hyle, and Jordan 2009). The dearth of Black students, in addition to some non-Black students' limited exposure to Blacks, contributes to this feeling.

Ayana told me about a more personal relationship. One of her housemates asked her to explain the stereotypical behavior of Black people.

I think it [students having stereotypes about Blacks] is pretty prevalent. People would like to think that it's not. But the closer you get to other races, then they start asking you questions and you feel like, 'Where did you come from?' Like one of the girls in the house I used to live in, we were cool; she was really nice and we talked quite a bit. Then she started asking me questions about how I eat watermelon, she said, 'Why do Black people put salt on watermelon?' I was like, 'I don't know.' Or she would ask, 'Did you grow up in the ghetto?' Just little questions like that, it was just random questions to ask in the first place, so it must come from some sort of stereotypical idea of what Black people do or how they are. (Ayana, native Black female, second-year student)

The hardest thing about college for her was "the atmosphere." She came from a predominantly African American neighborhood and felt she was a minority for the first time in college. When Ayana went home, she didn't have to worry about how she is perceived:

I didn't think about race when I was back home. I didn't think about how people look at me. Now [racism] is so much more real... Now when I go home, it's really nice to be home. You realize how relaxing it can be. (Ayana)

The campus was an uncomfortable environment for her, a place where she was seen as answerable for all the stereotypes that other students have about Blacks.

The combination of media-driven stereotypes and limited exposure to Blacks can elicit curiosity in non-Blacks. A few respondents came across non-Black students who wanted to befriend them *because* they were Black. Imani, a second-year student described meeting one of her roommates at the dorm:

When I met one of my roommates the day I moved in, she was like, 'Hi! I'm such-and-such, we're going to have so much fun together!' I'm looking at her like, 'Why do you think that?' Then as the weeks go by, I realize she listens to rap music, she likes Black guys, she likes the hip-hop culture, she likes the clubs. I don't like to do any of those things. So, no, we didn't have fun together. (Imani, native Black female, second-year student)

Her new roommate expected her to be interested in stereotypically Black culture.
Jasmin had a similar experience with an Asian student who had not met many Black people before.

> One Asian young man, and we had to talk about this, so he listens to Wu-Tang Clan... and I don't only listen to hip-hop and R & B, I listen to all kinds of music, and I'm not from the Bay either, and you know how they have the hyphy movement. So, every time they play E-40 [San Francisco Bay Area rapper] or something, he's like, 'Come on, get hyphy! You know how to get hyphy, teach me.' And I'm like, 'Wow, you assume that I know how to get hyphy? You assume that I know how to dance just because I am Black, and you haven't even seen me dance yet?' So I was like, 'Wow...' And he just seemed so happy to have a Black person in his life because he's listening to all this music. (Jasmin, native Black female, third-year student)

Respondents came across non-Black students who, perhaps because they were from racially homogenous neighborhoods and schools, held expectations of Blacks' preferences and abilities. These expectations may manifest as excitement when meeting a roommate or potential friend who is Black, but that excitement is misguided. In more cases, non-Black students' expectations led to prejudiced views and treatment.

Immigrant Blacks and native Blacks
Experiences of discrimination on campus can range from a random person asking what sport a Black student plays to a classmate showing concern that a Black student will not pull her weight in a group setting. The former scenario, a nameless student on campus acting in a subtly prejudiced way, was brought up by many respondents. Instances of subtle racism were reported in equal numbers by native Black (12 of 19) and immigrant Black (13 of 20) respondents. The latter scenario, interpersonal racism, was reported more often by native Blacks (18 of 19) than immigrant Blacks (13 of 20). In the statistical analysis, I reported native Blacks' higher incidence of reporting discrimination (Table 5.4, Model 1). However, when background factors are taken

into account, the significance of this relationship dissipates (Table 5.4, Model 2). This statistical finding, in addition to the small difference in the number of native versus immigrant Black interview respondents reporting discrimination, makes it unlikely that immigrant generation has a large and significant impact on perceiving discrimination.

The interview data show that immigrant and native Black students have similar experiences of discrimination at this college. As recounted earlier in this section, respondents from both groups talked about the myriad stereotypes that other students had about Blacks in general. Respondents from both groups discussed feeling uncomfortable on campus because they are Black. This discomfort stemmed from small acts of exclusion, such as other students staring at or avoiding them. Immigrant and native Black students were asked if they were athletes, suggesting that they were admitted to the university based on athletics rather than academics. Interpersonal interactions in the classroom were sometimes exercises in racial exclusion for Black students. On the whole, the phenomenon that emerged from the interview data was that in this academic arena, immigrant and native Blacks were not accepted as students.

Questioning Black students' academic identity
Black students are made to feel that they are not full members of the student body. I explore the interviewees' descriptions of how their place in the academic arena was questioned. Then I explore respondents' strategies to combat this questioning.

I begin with the subtle ways in which Black students are made to feel uncomfortable on campus. This can happen without words, perhaps with just a look. Titilayo, a Nigerian American student, recounts how her classmates were staring at her because they believed she didn't belong in a rigorous math class:

> Maybe this isn't what people are thinking, but maybe… I think of, like when you're one of the only few Black people in science and math classes and people just sort of look at you like, 'Do you belong here? This is Math 1B, this is Calculus. What are you doing here?' (Titilayo, Nigerian American female, second-year student)

She was tentative about her belief that students held prejudiced ideas about Black students. "Maybe this isn't what people are thinking," Titilayo said.

In contrast, Tekle, an Ethiopian student, was unequivocal about the looks he and his friends got, "There's discrimination on campus. There's a lot of discrimination going on. When you're walking with your friends, people just stare at you." (Tekle, Ethiopian male, second year student) In both cases, it was looks from others on campus that showed these respondents that they are not completely accepted as students.

Jasmin discussed how these looks created an atmosphere of tension for her:

> If there's a group of Black people that I'm with, and we're studying in a library, I feel like people look twice or stare because it's a group of Black people, as if it's unexpected... I feel like other people don't feel comfortable with the fact that I'm Black or they might discriminate against me because of that, and that makes me uncomfortable. (Jasmin, native Black female, third-year student)

She had an ethnically diverse network of friends on campus and the two student groups she belonged to were diverse as well. Jasmin had enmeshed herself in student life on this campus, yet she was made to feel as if she did not belong simply because she was studying with a group of Black students.

When others on campus give judgmental looks to Black students, it creates an uncomfortable environment. For the majority of respondents in this study, these experiences of prejudice extended to other subtle acts of discrimination that occurred in the public spaces of campus.

Abike, a Nigerian American respondent, said she had not experienced overt racism on campus, but she described how a mundane occurrence, walking down the main plaza of campus, is an exercise in exclusion. Students use the busy plaza as a place to hand out fliers for various student groups or events. Abike said:

> I never had anyone blatantly be racist or prejudice towards me, but like, there's stuff like if you walk down [the main plaza],

there's people who divert around you to pass out fliers or stuff like that, but no one says anything crazy to me.   (Abike, Nigerian American female, third-year student)

When she perceived that a member of a student group was choosing not to give a flier to her, she felt excluded. There were groups on campus, many groups, which did not view her as a potential member. Perhaps not coincidentally, Abike belonged to three campus groups, all of which are for Black or minority students.

Brandi, a native Black respondent, described the same situation and her reaction to it:

I just see small things like sometimes people will be passing out fliers on [main plaza] and they won't give me one. But most of the time they will, but one or two times. Or they'll think about it, they'll like pull it back. I'm like, "Ok" [surprise]. But I may or may not have wanted to go anyway. Most of the stuff they're handing out I probably wouldn't go to because I don't have time or it may or may not be of interest to me. But that didn't make me feel uncomfortable, I'd probably have to go look for a recycling bin anyway, to put it in. (Brandi, native Black female, first-year student)

She said this situation did not make her uncomfortable; however, in this subtle way, other students were saying that she was not welcome in their group or at their event.

One indirect form of prejudice that came up often in the interviews was people asking if the respondents were athletes. This finding is consistent with a similar qualitative study at a predominantly White college (Feagin1992). The underlying prejudice is that the only reason a Black person would be at this college is on scholarship for sports. Ozioma, a first-year Nigerian American student, recounted this experience:

I was walking down the street and I had on [her high school] track and field sweatshirt. I don't run track here [her college]. And someone said, 'Oh, you're a runner. [college cheer]!' Things like that, little, little things like that add up and you start to realize, you hear other people going through it. We have the same experiences. Little things, they don't have to say it, they can just act that way towards you. Sometimes people think you're paranoid. You try to think that they don't think that way, but some people do. (Ozioma, Nigerian American female, first-year student)

She believed this was a small incident; perhaps it could have been construed differently, but all of these small incidences and the common experience of other Black students, make it evident that Black students are being treated differently because of their race. Other students do not see Blacks as academic peers. Ozioma was mistaken for a college athlete and understood the meaning behind the "little" incident:

A lot of people think that because you're Black and you go to a good college, you go to [her college], people think you're an athlete. You get that stigma a lot. It's hard to prove yourself, that you do belong here, that you are on par with everyone else. People look at you, 'You probably got here through athletics.' (Ozioma)

The stereotype that Black students are on athletic scholarships automatically puts them in a position of disadvantage. They must, from the start, prove that they are true students.

A similar experience was recounted by Itunu, a young Nigerian woman. The incident she described occurred as she arrived on campus:

Freshmen orientation, my group, we were going on asking each other, 'Why did you choose [college]?' And before it came to my turn, somebody just made some ignorant comment like, 'Oh, what sport do you play?' And I said, 'Uh, I played track in high school, but it has nothing to do with me here. What is the connection?' She's like, 'Oh, I thought you were here on an athletic scholarship.' (Itunu, Nigerian female, third-year student)

Itunu held a fellowship that covered all of her academic and living expenses for six years of undergraduate education. She described her reaction:

So I calmly explained to her, 'No, I have a full-ride.' I said it with a cocky attitude, but at that point, I had to tell her, 'I'm not here on an athletic scholarship, I'm here on an academic scholarship. I don't have mommy and daddy paying for me like you do.' I think I shouldn't have said that, but I was already kind of emotional at that point. (Itunu)

These ignorant remarks can be unsettling for students. Others on campus are questioning their identity as students, which can shake them emotionally. Itunu, like Ozioma who was presumed to be on the college track team, also knew people who have encountered the same situation. She told me about one friend in particular:

I remember this one guy freshmen year, he's tall; he fits the role for a basketball player. Nobody knew who he was, but they were like, 'Oh, do you play [college] basketball?' He was like, 'No, I don't.' He said that so many times. I was like, 'Wow, this bad. You can't have a Black man in college unless he's playing a sport?' (Itunu)

In these ways, Black students' presence on campus is questioned. These individual instances build up and Black students become aware that they must continually defend their status as "regular" students, not athletes.

Jahzara, a native Black student, said she tries to keep an open mind about others, "I'm optimistic and I give people the benefit of the doubt, but at the same time, racism is so ubiquitous." She told me about others questioning her place at the university:

I got into [college] without Affirmative Action. People told me, 'Oh, you got in because you're Black.' No, I didn't. But that's what people think. That's what people say to you! When you're a Black student on campus, people ask you, 'Are you an athlete?' There's things that Black students have to deal with that no one else does. When other people come from all-white schools or a school where there might not have been that many Black people or minorities, they're missing

that picture. They don't get enlightened. (Jahzara, native
Black female, third-year student)

Other respondents had similar experiences of being told they were in
college through Affirmative Action. As I discussed in Chapter 3,
Affirmative Action has not been used in UC admissions since 1997,
more than ten years before the interviews in this study. Despite a
decade of no race-based admissions, Black students are still seen as
beneficiaries of Affirmative Action.

When non-Black students have lowered academic expectations for
Black students, it can affect the way they interact with Black students.
These prejudiced views have academic consequences for Black
students. Experiences that were mentioned by many interviewees (16
of 39) were: being excluded when the class formed groups and
encountering prejudiced classmates while working in groups. These
findings of being left out in the college classroom setting are consistent
with similar studies (Davis, et al. 2004, Crim 1998). In the present
study, there was no difference in these experiences in terms of
immigrant generation.

One common experience and fear is being excluded when classes
break up into small groups or partners. Aaliyah believed some of her
classmates were not aware of their own prejudices.

It does affect a lot, even if it's not done consciously. In my
Psychology discussion, we had to do group work in one of the
classes and everyone kind of looked at me and two other
Black kids in the discussion, and looking like, 'Oh, I don't
really want them in my group.' (Aaliyah, native Black female,
first-year student)

She lamented the persistence of discrimination at the supposedly liberal
campus. Yet, personally, she tried to look past it.

If I think about it [prejudice], it will always be a weight on
me... In this semester, we read Barak Obama's book and he
was like, 'If a girl would mention how much she likes Stevie
Wonder or ask me if I play basketball, why do such comments
put me on edge?' So, I realized that not everything is meant

as an insult. I just try to take that guard down, not being so paranoid about things. I've learned a lot how to do that. (Aaliyah)

For her own sake, she practiced generosity in her interpretation of potentially prejudiced remarks. She believed she could avoid the stress that thinking about prejudice would cause. Black students start from a position of lowered status; they are the unwanted group members or lab partners. They may surprise prejudiced classmates with sharp answers or gain their trust over the course of many classes together. However, their initial standing is one of disadvantage.

Tekle who talked about being stared at in the public spaces on campus, described how racism played out for him in the classroom and the dorm. The classroom would fall silent when he would speak. He recounted his experience of trying unsuccessfully to find a partner in a lab:

> My first Chemistry class, the lab was worse than the class. We had to do a project. The GSI [graduate student instructor] said, 'Ok, you guys have to be in partners.' I was just by myself. Everybody jumped on to find a partner to partner. Even the people who were sitting in front of me, went around the classroom to find a partner. This one person didn't come, so they were my partner. (Tekle, Ethiopian male, immigrated to the U.S. at 11 years old, second-year student)

Other students seemed to question Tekle's identity as a student. Classmates actively avoided him when asked to pair up for a project. Tekle experienced prejudice in his dorm as well:

> There were two particular students who live right across from the elevator. These two are white and Asian American... they came to the room, they knocked and said 'hi' and stuff like that. And I said, 'Hi. How are you guys doing?' And the white girl, she said, 'We thought you were a gangster, so we were scared of you.' I was like, 'Whoa. Where does that come from? What's going on?' I didn't expect that at all from anyone that I've ever met, anyone that I've talked to,

anyone. That right there, obviously there's an image of me, something, you think I'm a gangster... I'm like, 'What's going on here? You have to see a Black person as a gangster?' That disappointed me, that they thought of me like that. Plus, the Asian American girl, she's in my science classes. I didn't really expect that, coming from her, at all. (Tekle)

The stereotypes that non-Black students have about Blacks may persist, despite living in the same dorm and taking the same classes. It is clear that Tekle's race is his master status (as described in the seminal piece by Hughes 1945). Some of his classmates and dormmates see only his race. In their minds, the fact that he is Black conflicts with the fact that he is a student. They therefore doubt his academic ability or question his identity as a student. Being a classmate in science classes or a neighbor in the dorm pales in comparison to being Black.

Tekle's experiences with subtle racism while walking around on campus and in the classroom, and with blatant racism in his dorm each contribute to a generalized and omnipresent threat of discrimination. Despite working in the same group for the semester, Ezinne, a Nigerian American, said one group member would not accept her contributions.

This lab I was taking in Bio, everything we do is in groups. You don't pick your groups, either way I would have still been the only Black person in the group because I was the only Black person in that lab. My group, it wasn't the whole group, but one guy in the group, everyone else was cool. He wasn't a bad person, but I would say the answer and he would keep on looking in the book, and I would say it again and he would keep on looking. I would say it four times, and he'd be like, 'Oh, yada, yada, yada' [as if reading from the textbook]. I would look at him like, 'Didn't I just say that?' He doesn't think my answers are correct. It probably was because I'm Black. I don't know if his ears just closed up when I spoke. He would be like, 'Let me just make sure.' (Ezinne, U.S.-born Nigerian American, second-year student)

Even though the rest of the group members were "cool," Ezinne felt undermined because her contributions were continually questioned by one student.

Experiences with prejudiced classmates can make Black students feel that partnering with non-Blacks is risky, that they are exposing themselves to prejudiced treatment. Kim, introduced earlier in this chapter, talked about having to convince her study group members that she was a serious student.

> I kind of always feel like people don't expect me to do as well just because we're African American... advisors, and classmates, but in a way that they don't realize they're doing it. If you're in a study group, no one really asks me. If I happen to do something wrong, it's like, 'Oh, don't worry, you don't have to understand this.' It's like, no, I want to understand it. That doesn't make any sense. Why wouldn't I want to learn?" (Kim, native Black female, second-year student)

Kim echoed an idea that Aaliyah mentioned, that these people might not be aware of their prejudices. They took one mistake as proof that Kim was not a real student and was therefore exempt from learning. She gave the following specific example:

> The lab report said, '0.5' but the bottle that we were getting the solution from said, '0.475' but I went off of '0.5' and I told other people next to me that. When they were getting their numbers wrong, they were trying to figure out why. Then he realized, 'Oh, the bottle says 0.475.' Then he's like, 'Yeah, *someone* told me the wrong number.' And he had this really effed up attitude the whole time, but he never said anything to me. Even though he never said anything to me, '*Someone.*' Don't patronize me like that. If you have something to say... I said I was sorry... After that, I just started doing labs with the Black girl... My [chemistry] lab, first I was doing labs with everyone and then I just ended up with the only other Black person in class. (Kim)

The lowered expectations that other students might have for Black students creates a high-stakes atmosphere for Black students. If they make one mistake then they are living out the negative stereotypes that others may have about them. The fear of fulfilling a negative stereotype has been shown to have deleterious effects on academic performance (Steele and Aronson 1995).

Some immigrant Black respondents (7 of 20) talked about discrimination by professors or graduate student instructors (GSI's). A comparable number of native Black respondents (8 of 19) had similar experiences. On this campus of over 20,000 undergraduates, many classes, even upper-division classes, are large lectures with smaller discussion sections. The sections are led by GSI's, so most students only see these professors in lecture halls with hundreds of other students. Some students choose to attend professors' office hours where they may have an opportunity to interact with the professor one-on-one or, in the case of most science and math classes, with a few other students. I grouped professors and GSI's together as instructors because they are both in positions of power in the classroom and in terms of grading students. In fact, GSI's do much of the grading for large classes.

Makeda, an Ethiopian student, estimated that one-third to one-half of professors is racially prejudiced against Black students:

> A lot of professors would automatically... not all of them, I've had some good ones, but some of them automatically assume that you're stupid or that you're not as smart. So when you ask questions, I ask a lot of questions and stuff, they would not take my questions seriously until I proved that I was smart or something and then they're like, 'Ok, well, I guess I have to answer her questions.' But that's not in all, that's probably in one-half to one-third of the classes, and then the other one-half to two-thirds of the classes were good, the professors were nice and everything. (Makeda, U.S.-born Ethiopian female, third-year student)

In the follow-up questionnaire, she said she had been treated unfairly by a GSI in the year since the interview. During the interview, she gave me a specific example of a professor who voiced his lower expectations of her.

> He had a diagnostic questionnaire and it was one Chemistry question and I wrote my answer and he just made my answer sound so stupid. And it turns out it wasn't even really stupid, it just wasn't what he was looking for... He's like, 'You can stay in the class but I think you're going to fail.' And I got an A in that class and eventually he answered all of my questions. (Makeda)

Makeda recounted this experience in response to a question about experiencing discrimination from professors or GSI's. The Chemistry professor discouraged her from taking his class because he didn't believe she was academically prepared. He based his assessment on a diagnostic questionnaire, but Makeda believed that he didn't give her answer a fair look. He was also not prepared to help her succeed in the class. She believed that his dismissive attitude was based on her race.

Of the 15 interviewees who said they experienced discrimination from instructors, 14 mentioned strategies for success, such as creating relationships with instructors, demonstrating earnestness, and proving academic skills. A Nigerian American student, Dele, explained how he may start from a disadvantaged position, but works steadily to change that:

> In terms of GSI's, once I get that relationship with them, I feel like they trust I'm a hard-working individual and I'm doing everything that I can. Once I build a relationship with them, then that thought that African American students came from bad schools and need special academic help is erased, I hope. I feel like, I'm here, I'm in class, but I have to go farther than the person sitting on my right. (Dele, U.S.-born Nigerian American, second-year student)

He began classes knowing he had to prove he is capable. His strategy was to create a relationship with the GSI by demonstrating his perseverance and abilities.

Most of the respondents who encountered discrimination were determined to prove themselves as valid students. Maurice made the Track team after matriculating to college. He told me about his strategy for combating prejudice.

Sometimes the professor thinks, 'Oh, athlete?' You know, then they [professors] don't like him [student athlete]. I just make sure that I am on top of everything all the time... For every professor this semester, I went up and talked to them the first day of class so that they know my name, so that they know who I am, so that they know what my work ethic is. My parents always taught me that that was the way you're supposed to handle that. Part of the reason they told me that is because in some instances, you're going to be in the case where people are going to assume that because you're Black you're not going to be as good. (Maurice, native Black male, first-year student)

Black students have strategies for handling instructors who may be prejudiced against them. At first, Maurice said he introduced himself to professors because they might think that he is not a serious student because he is on the Track team. Later he acknowledged that part of the reason is to mitigate lowered expectations that instructors may have about Black students. He is motivated to prove himself as a legitimate student in order to combat the stereotypes about Black men in college: that they are not interested in or capable of the academic work.

Bradley, a second-year student, said he didn't dwell on what his classmates thought of him, but he participated in class to show the instructor that he was conscientious.

A teacher might show favoritism. They'll explain a problem; they won't explain it to me as fully as they would to someone else. That's happened to me before, like GSI's. Like, I was in a business class and I was the only, I think I was the only Black person in that section, in the discussion. I felt like maybe people doubt me. I really have the attitude where I can't worry about what people think. I just have to get my grade, show a good effort. I participated, spoke and things

like that.   And my GSI saw it and I did good in class.
(Bradley, native Black male, second-year student)

He demonstrated his seriousness and diligence to his instructor, and was rewarded with a good grade. However, because he was Black, he began the class with a disadvantage.

James said he has encountered discrimination but ignored it. Even if he received a slightly lower grade because an instructor was prejudiced, he would shrug it off:

> If I'm on the borderline and say the person's racist, they give me the C+ instead of the B-, I really don't care. I think it all evens itself out in the end. I wouldn't lose sleep over it... If he changes my grade from an A to an F, I may have to say something then. [laughs] (James, native Black male, first-year student)

Unlike the previous respondents, Sherice was not able to overlook discrimination from her professor:

> I remember my first year, I took [introductory science course] and I introduced myself to the professor during class, after class the first day. He was like, 'Oh, are you an athlete?' I'm like, 'No.' I guess the athletes come in the beginning of class and say, 'I'm an athlete, I'm not going to be here, blah, blah, blah.' But I was just introducing myself because you hear, 'Go to office hours. Meet your professor.' So I was trying to do it. It was really awkward to me... I never went to office hours [for that professor] after that. I was discouraged. If you're going to stereotype me like that, I don't want to go anymore. (Sherice, native Black female, third-year student)

At the time of the interview Sherice was in her third year in school and said she thought about transferring to another college "all the time." At the time of the follow-up questionnaire one year later, she was still enrolled at the same school and had a B-/B average. Although Sherice became discouraged and avoided the instructor, she made it to her fourth year in college and was doing well academically.

When Black students speak out in class, they can sometimes tell that their thoughtful questions or intelligent answers are unexpected. Tekle described a classroom situation:

> I see this a lot, when I speak, the whole room is dead silence, compared to when other people speak, there's chitting chatting going on, just normal. When I raise my hand and say something, it's dead silent, like, 'Whoa, what is he going to say now?' Participation is what discussion class is for, so I try to participate. I raise my hand, say some things. It's dead silence. People don't expect me to say something. They expect I'll just sit there in class then walk out. When I say something, they're surprised. (Tekle, Ethiopian male, immigrated to the U.S. at 11 years old, second-year student)

Tekle was acting as any good student would, yet his classmates are surprised that he would participate in class.

Nicole, an immigrant Black student who identified as Nigerian and African American, started by saying, "I don't think they [other students] know they have lowered expectations [of me]." That is, perhaps non-Black students are not even aware of their own prejudices. She went on to say, "I just think it's funny to hear, like let's say you answer a really difficult question and people are like [gasp], like surprised." (Nicole, U.S.-born of Nigerian immigrant parents, first-year student) Her intelligence took her classmates by surprise.

Negative reaction to discrimination
The majority of interviewees who said they had experienced discrimination on campus went on to describe adaptive strategies for succeeding academically. Six respondents talked about experiences of discrimination that lead to negative academic responses. For example, Sherice, the Black student who did not go back to her professor's office hours because he had assumed that she was an athlete. Two respondents went a step further and had dropped classes after encountering prejudiced classmates. And three Black students said they avoided speaking in class because they were insecure about the worth of their contributions. These students acknowledged that their

grades would be negatively affected by their lack of participation in class discussions.

An immigrant Black student, Abike said that she, along with several other students, added the class late. When obtaining permission from the professor, she was the only one who received a warning that she could not miss any more classes. She ended up dropping the class. Abike talked about the discrimination that Black students encounter on campus and said that as a result:

> A lot of people from my year are not here anymore, like just are not here... People just disappeared, they're like gone. There's a lot of stuff you have to deal with, going to this school. School is not just school anymore when you get here. It's not because of the 'real world,' it's not any of that, it's stuff that goes on in this school. (Abike, U.S.-born Nigerian American, third-year student)

In the follow-up questionnaire, she reported experiencing discrimination from professors, students, and the administration since the time of the interview. Although she talked about other Black students dropping out and felt that discrimination was continual and from many sources, she persevered. At the time of the follow-up questionnaire, Abike indicated that she was enrolled as a fourth-year, full-time student and had a B/B+ average.

Shanice had a similar story of persevering through difficulty. First she talked about how difficult it had been for her to participate in class. It was apparent during the interview that she had a stutter. I asked her what was the hardest thing about college so far and her response was:

> The hardest thing about going to [her college] is having confidence. I know ever since I got here, my already-low confidence is super-duper low. I started stuttering now. Before, I spoke at my graduation, I spoke at my fifth grade graduation, and all these functions in front of people. But when I got here, I couldn't even talk here in class really. I start getting sweaty and I really doubt my abilities and people can tell when I write papers. So I never really participate fully

because I'm afraid people are going to think I'm stupid.
(Shanice, native Black female, third-year student)

Her stutter developed when she reached college. The root of her insecurity was a feeling that she was conspicuous as the only Black student in class.

> I was like, 'Oh, I'm the only Black person in this class or the only Black female.' And I'm like, 'Oh my god, I just won't say anything.' It would be really bad if we had group projects. I remember once, I had had a group project, I didn't say anything, the whole time! [laughs] I'd just agree with what my partner says. It was so dumb. (Shanice)

On the questionnaire before the interview, she rated her academic ability as "Somewhat below average" in comparison to that of the average student at her college. Only two other interviewees rated themselves as "Somewhat below average;" The vast majority of interviewees rated their academic ability as "Average" (n = 19) or "Somewhat above average" (n = 15), with two rating themselves "Well above average." Despite Shanice's apprehensions about her abilities, she said she is gaining confidence and believes she can succeed.

> I'd be like, 'Oh, I can't make it. I can't graduate.' But as each semester goes by, I'm like, 'Oh, I can do it!' I'm past the half-way point. Upper-divs are more specific and easier to understand because you focus on narrow topics. There was a time when I had an A in a rhetoric class this semester and I'm like, 'Wow!' (Shanice)

On the follow-up questionnaire, she indicated that she had a B/B+ average. By persevering, Shanice believed she would graduate, perhaps even excel.

Another strategy is to use the Black student community as a buffer against potential discrimination. Nnenna felt that some of her classmates thought she had poor academic abilities because she was Black. She had dropped out of science courses because she found it difficult to work with prejudiced classmates.

It's most apparent in lab, I'd say... I had to team up with this other girl. She was like rushing through the experiment and was looking at me like I was stupid... Yeah, I guess that's why I dropped out of them [courses with labs]. (Nnenna, U.S.-born Nigerian female, third-year student)

She subsequently discovered a support program on campus for minorities who are in the sciences. She was able to find other Black and racial minority students who understood her situation and could team up with her.

In labs, I'll wonder, 'Who am I going to pair up with?' Luckily, there are people that I know. I've always made sure that my friends were in lab with me... I guess I take precautions to make sure that [working with a prejudiced classmate] doesn't happen. (Nnenna)

Although Nnenna initially struggled, she found a resource to help her succeed academically. In Chapter 4, I explored the academic benefits of membership in the Black student community.

The students who described negative reactions to discriminatory treatment continued in school and did well. Thus, it can be difficult to gauge the actual impact of a hostile racial environment on academic performance and outcomes. The statistical data suggest that there is not a direct relationship, but the qualitative data describe a complex interaction, with Black students finding novel ways to engage in a threatening arena.

Academically adaptive strategies
Expectations and stereotypes that non-Black students have about Blacks create a pressured, high-stakes atmosphere for Black students. This is especially true when assumptions about Black students' abilities are brought into the classroom. Black students may react by attempting to prove stereotypes wrong (Davis, et al. 2004). When I asked about the stereotypes that others may have about Black students, Latoya, a native Black student, said:

That we're confrontational, that we might be a little bit less intelligent than other people. I think we have to represent ourselves in a very different manner. If we're in class, we always have to represent ourselves in a professional manner, so show we're not slackers, we definitely can do the work... I think instantly, right off the bat, as African Americans we have to prove that we're not lazy, prove those stereotypes wrong. I always sit in front of the class to show the teacher I'm very focused and I always read and I always have my books with me. I always reference the books so they know I'm not the type of person that didn't read... Just being the only minority, you feel like you have the obligation of... proving stereotypes wrong. (Latoya, native Black female, second-year student)

Latoya had specific strategies to dispel the low expectations that professors, graduate student instructors, and other students might have of her.

Robert, who was presented earlier regarding negative racial stereotypes, described the atmosphere of his classes:

It's just this intuition. It might be the look, the approach. Just the way that the environment and the energy is inside the class. There is a bit of a pressure, but you don't really let it get to you... I might participate more in class. I might do more to stand out. Well, I'm already standing out, why don't I stand out even more. (Robert, native Black male, first-year student)

Robert had a hard time putting his finger on exactly what was making him uncomfortable, but he felt the pressure to disprove negative stereotypes. He spoke out in class, a strategy many respondents also employed.

This was true for Nicole, mentioned earlier in this chapter. She talked about the disadvantaged position that Black students start from:

I've done that before where I'm like, 'I know one of the reasons you think I'm not as smart as you is because of my skin color and because you thought I was an athlete and I couldn't be as smart as everybody else and I'm going to prove you wrong.' You're doing twice as much to get half as far. So, I'm answering all these questions [in class] to prove to people, 'Listen, I'm intelligent.' And it's also partially to prove to myself that I know the coursework. (Nicole, U.S.-born of Nigerian immigrant parents, first-year student)

Her strategy for dealing with prejudiced classmates is beneficial to her academically, but it is a constant struggle. In the follow-up questionnaire, Nicole indicated that, in the year since the interview, she had experienced discrimination from another student. Prejudice can seem unrelenting for Black students.

James had talked about "shrugging off" discriminatory treatment from instructors. He went on to describe a strategy to handle the negative stereotypes that students and professors have of Blacks. He always sat in the front of the classroom, in each course, at every class meeting:

I feel like being Black, you really have to do that [talk to professors outside of class] sometimes. I sit in the front row for all classes... You sit in the back row, people assume things, especially when you're Black. When you're in a place where you're the vast minority and there's as much negative connotations about you as much as there is about Black people, sit in the back row and it's like, 'Oh, typical Black student, you're not paying attention, you don't really care about your education.' You sit in the front row, you make a statement, like, 'I'm here every class taking notes.' And you're more noticeable when you're Black, sitting in the front row. All my teachers know my name. (James, native Black male, first-year student)

James had strategies in the classroom and also made it a point to speak with his professors outside of class. Because of his assertive academic approach, all of his instructors knew him. Like Nicole, he reported on his follow-up questionnaire that he had experienced discrimination from a student. He was continually battling prejudice.

A second-year student, Chika, said her classmates' lowered expectations became apparent when she participated in class:

> It's always nice when you ask a really smart question and they get taken back a little bit by it, like, 'Huh?' I'm like, 'Oh, so you thought I was dumb!' I like proving people wrong because I know that when I walk into a class, the first thing people think about me is not, 'Oh, she's going to be really smart in this class.' Maybe it's just in my head, but I think that people don't think, 'Oh, she's going to be the A student in this class.' I feel like I like proving people wrong, but that's how I learn, I have to be involved in lectures. (Chika, Nigerian female, immigrated to the U.S. at 16 years old, second-year student)

She felt that her classmates had low expectations for her academic ability. Part of Chika's motivation for participating in class was to defy their expectations, but she also saw the real academic benefit of it. Black students' strategies for battling lowered expectations and negative stereotypes are sometimes academically adaptive. This is not to say that discrimination in any way aids students, but that, perhaps through years in this threatening setting, Black college students have developed tactics to handle prejudice and succeed in the academic arena.

In the statistical analysis, discrimination was not significantly related to academic outcomes. A possible explanation emerges from the interview data: Black students at this flagship campus had developed an arsenal of strategies that allowed them to maintain their status in the academic arena, even as that status was called into question. The respondents in this study explained the many tactics they employ to prove and maintain their identity as students. Their academically adaptive strategies may compensate for the negative effect of discrimination on their educational outcomes.

DISCUSSION

Immigrant and native Black students report discrimination on campus with similar frequency. According to the statistical analysis, when socioeconomic status is taken into account, there is no difference in Black students' perceptions of discrimination by immigrant generation (Table 5.4, Model 2). Results from the interview data bolster this finding. Immigrant and native Black students describe instances of discrimination on campus in similar numbers. I add this finding to the mounting evidence of a *Black student experience*. In Chapter 3, I found similar rates of intellectual integration and a common Black identity for immigrant and native Blacks. A cohesive Black student community, bridging immigrant generations, was described in Chapter 4 along with similar rates of social integration and interethnic interaction. In the next chapter, I will explore if family immigration history affects Black student graduation rates.

Thus, Ogbu's (1991) theory that voluntary immigrants are less likely to perceive discrimination is not borne out. However, the present study is not a direct test of Ogbu's theory since immigrants and second-generation immigrants are conflated in the statistical analysis. Waters (1999) found that persistence structural racism eroded immigrant optimism over time. While Black immigrants from African and the Caribbean may be able to maintain positive attitudes in the face of structural racism, this may not be true for their U.S.-born children. On the college campus, Blacks are underrepresented. In the academic domain, Blacks are besieged by negative stereotypes. It is not surprising that second-generation Black immigrants experience discrimination at similar rates and react to it in similar ways to native Blacks.

Black students differ from Asian, Chicano/Latino, and White students in their perceptions of the racial climate of UC campuses. On the whole, they are less likely to believe that students are respected regardless of race or ethnicity. Even after taking family characteristics, high school performance, and campus selectivity into account, Black students' perceptions of discrimination are significantly higher than White students'. In addition, this relationship remains significant when considering only the interview site. These results bolster the findings of other studies suggesting that the crucial cut of the color line in the U.S. is between Black and non-Black (Lee and Bean 2007, Sears, Fu, Henry, and Bui 2007), pointing to a *unique Black student experience* in college.

Feeling respected on campus is not related to college grades or graduation. Black students' negative view of the racial climate on campus do not (in the statistically models) appear to directly affect academic performance or outcomes. However, the prevalence of Black students' experiences with discrimination, as evidenced by the quantitative *and* interview data, suggest that there is more to the story. The interview data provide a glimpse into the world of Black college students at this university. Looks from others on campus and subtle acts of exclusion create an unwelcoming environment for Black students. Through these "small" incidents and less innocuous acts, such as asking if a Black student is an athlete, others call into question the validity of Blacks' identity as students. Negative academic stereotypes are constantly in the background for Black students, creating a high-stakes atmosphere in which they are terrified of living out those negative stereotypes and desperate to prove those same stereotypes wrong.

These findings resonate with the extant literature documenting the negative effects of discrimination on academic engagement (Schmader, Major, and Gramzow 2001, Wong Eccles, and Sameroff 2003), grades (Steele 1997, Steele and Aronson 1995, Smedley, Myers, and Harrell 1993), and institutional commitment (Harper and Hurtado 2007, Cabrera, et al. 1999). Yet Black students enumerate the adaptive academic strategies that they employ: working hard, speaking in class, giving others the benefit of the doubt, "shrugging it off," getting to know instructors and classmates, sitting in the front of the class, and the list goes on. Black students need these strategies because they are constantly faced with the situation in which they must interact with their non-Black classmates. Their experiences of non-Black classmates avoiding or actively excluding them from groups have made the need to join a group one that is fraught with apprehension for Black students. Once in these groups, Black students feel they must continually defend their status as serious contributors to the group. The constant and omnipresent assault on Black students' identity as students has led some to question whether they are paranoid about discrimination. Then they add up all the "small" incidents and the similar experiences of their co-ethnic peers, and many see that they are not paranoid. There truly are prejudiced students and even instructors at their college. Black students encounter instructors who also question their identity as valid students. In a few cases, Black students react to discrimination in a way that has a negative impact on their academic progress.

The non-significance of discrimination on graduation belies the true experiences of Black students on college campuses. I suggest that those Black students who have made it to a University of California campus have acquired adaptive strategies that mitigate the deleterious effects of discrimination on academic performance. As described in the qualitative data, Black students have a deep bench of tactics to cope with racial discrimination from instructors and classmates. It is these compensating mechanisms that account for the non-significance of discrimination on graduation.

CONCLUSION

Both the quantitative and qualitative findings point to a distinct Black student experience on college campuses. Black students feel less respected than students of other ethnicities and are continually defending their identity as students. Within the Black community, there appears to be a common Black student experience. As with the chapters on ethnic diversity, social capital, and educational attainment, the results of this chapter on discrimination show that there is little difference in the college experience and outcomes for immigrant and native Black students. Although there is no statistical relationship between discrimination and academic performance or outcomes, the interview data clearly show the toll that discrimination takes on Black students. They must employ academically adaptive strategies just to prove that they have a place in the classroom.

CHAPTER 6

Educational Attainment

RELEVANT LITERATURE

Differential achievement by immigrant generation

Based on the literature on immigrants in education, researchers expect that immigrant Blacks will be overrepresented among Black college students. Two reasons emerge from the extant literature: socioeconomic and cultural explanations. The overrepresentation of immigrant Blacks may be attributed to the fact that immigrant Blacks, in general, have greater education and income than native Blacks. This explanation allows for native and immigrant Blacks to have the same probability of matriculating to and graduating from college. Cultural explanations, on the other hand, posit an immigrant advantage and predict that, controlling for socioeconomic variables, immigrant Blacks will still have a higher probability of going to college. Two such theories, which I will discuss below, are: voluntary and involuntary minorities (Ogbu 1991) and segmented assimilation theory (Portes and Zhou 1993).

Tinto's model of intellectual integration (1975, 1987) points to the importance of institutional effects on college student attrition. When this theory of college student attrition is applied to the population in this study, we should expect no difference between native and immigrant Black students' graduation rates. Students who feel they belong at the campus will be more likely to persist and graduate. Given the common experience that most Black students have on the predominantly White college campus (Willie 2003), regardless of family immigration history (Smith and Moore 2000), this theory predicts the convergence of their graduation rates.

Socioeconomic explanations of differential academic attainment
The overrepresentation of immigrant Blacks among Black college students has been documented in the literature (Massey, et al. 2007, Glick and White 2004, Hagy and Staniec 2002); as have the socioeconomic advantages of Black African immigrants (Djamba 1999, Dodoo 1997). Income and education drive the overrepresentation of immigrant Blacks in college. In fact, a recent study showed, when controlling for background differences, such as family socioeconomic status, type of high school, and family structure, there is no difference between immigrant and native Black college attendance (Bennett and Lutz 2009). Often, social scientists acknowledge the effect of socioeconomic factors while also pointing to cultural factors.

Cultural explanations of differential academic attainment
Ogbu (1991) originally developed the theory of involuntary and voluntary minorities to the diverse educational outcomes of minority groups and in order to explain the crucial differences in education among these groups. In this study, the two groups, immigrant Black and native Black, have equal educational attainment: all the respondents are students in the same university system. However, when interview respondents at one campus talk about immigrant and native Blacks, they emphasize cultural differences between the two groups, echoing Ogbu's theory.

Ogbu (1991; Ogbu and Simons1998) argues that African Americans, who are involuntary minorities, have a different historical and societal situation than voluntary immigrants, such as today's Black immigrants. The terms of incorporation of a minority group affect how each group responds to discriminatory treatment.

Immigrants choose America as an alternative to their home country. In comparison with their minority peers in their home country, the immigrants have better opportunities. This results in a positive dual frame of reference, wherein the U. S. appears to offer more and better opportunities than their home country. In the voluntary immigrant's mind, hard work and education will lead to advancement. Any discriminatory treatment is seen as temporary and surmountable.

In contrast, involuntary minorities are in their present situation because of historical situations such as slavery or colonization. They have a negative dual frame of reference, comparing their situation with that of white Americans and seeing that they are not afforded the same opportunities because of their race. Discriminatory treatment is viewed as a permanent manifestation of oppression. Ogbu (2004; Fordham and Ogbu 1986) claims that involuntary minorities develop identities in opposition to the dominant group and don't believe that education or hard work can help them advance. According to this theory, Black immigrants and their children will fare better academically, socially, and economically than African Americans.

Researchers have challenged oppositional theory, presenting empirical evidence that African American students have high academic aspirations (Hauser and Anderson 1991, Ainsworth-Darnell and Downey 1998, Kao and Tienda 1998). However, this critique of oppositional theory has an important flaw. The relationship between educational aspirations and actual attainment is not direct. Without information, guidance, and motivation, aspirations to college may not result in tangible academic gains (Carter 2005, Schneider and Stevenson 1999). Perhaps native Blacks do not have an oppositional stance toward education, but even high educational aspirations will not ensure that native Blacks will have high educational attainment.

The overrepresentation of immigrant Blacks in higher education can be understood in terms of immigrant minorities and involuntary minorities. I apply this theory to findings from the qualitative data and find differing frames of reference for native versus immigrant Blacks.

While the theory of involuntary and immigrant minorities can be applied to immigrant versus native Black differences, segmented assimilation theory addresses differences among immigrant groups. Segmented assimilation theory does not directly speak to the experiences and outcomes of native minorities.

Portes and Zhou (1993) offer segmented assimilation theory as an alternative to straight-line assimilation theory. Based on research on early 20th-century immigration to America, straight-line assimilation theory dominated models of immigrant outcomes and incorporation for decades. Straight-line assimilation, or classic assimilation, postulates that over several generations immigrant families will assimilate into mainstream American culture and experience academic gains (Gordon 1964). Alba and Nee (2003) offer a reconceptualization of assimilation theory, arguing its relevance to many post-1965 immigrants and their progeny.

Segmented assimilation adds complexity to the classical assimilation theory by suggesting that immigrant groups have diverse outcomes; some remain within their ethnic community, perhaps selectively acculturating into mainstream society and enjoying academic success, while other groups may become part of the minority underclass and prematurely drop out of the educational system. Remaining within the co-ethnic community confers academic benefits when that community has a positive stance towards education (Portes and Rumbaut 2001, Bankston and Zhou, Waters 1999, Kao and Tienda 1998).

Family or ethnic community social capital is a useful concept when applying segmented assimilation theory to this study. Immigrant groups with strong norms of educational achievement create an atmosphere of high academic expectations for second-generation immigrants (Feliciano 2006). Qualitative results are in line with segmented assimilation theory if immigrant Black students should report strong norms enforcing academic success from their families and co-ethnic community. Segmented assimilation theory has an implicit assumption that native Blacks from economically-depressed areas will have an oppositional culture (Fordham and Ogbu 1986).

Along with Ogbu's concepts of involuntary and voluntary minorities, segmented assimilation offer cultural explanations of the disparity in college-going between native and immigrant Blacks. I asked each respondent to describe the trajectories of their Black childhood and high school friends. As I mentioned earlier, the qualitative data is limited in its applicability to the question of college-going. The information about respondents' Black friends is problematic from a sampling and data collection point of view. However, these data speak to the narratives that Blacks have about differences between immigrant and native Blacks. Respondents can speak to the differences in frames of reference, and family and community academic expectations.

Intellectual integration of Black students in college
The key components of Tinto's (1975, 1993) theory of college student retention hinges upon social and intellectual integration into the university. In Chapter 4, I found that social integration was not a significant predictor of Black college student graduation, although it

was an important factor for White students. The other component of Tinto's theory, intellectual integration, was introduced in Chapter 3. Intellectual integration is the alignment of the student's values with the perceived values of the university. It occurs when the student feels respected and supported within the university, when the student feels a sense of belonging to the institution.

Empirical studies have demonstrated the link between Black college students' sense of belonging to the university and their academic performance and retention (Fletcher 2012; Walton and Cohen 2011, 2007; Dovidio, et al. 2001; Allen 1992). Researchers have also found that Black students are less likely to feel belongingness in a predominantly White institution (Dovidio, et al. 2001, Allen 1992). The present study can speak to both of these points as well as address potential differences in immigrant versus native Black students' intellectual integration. Scholarly work in this area suggests that Black students have similar experiences on campus, regardless of family immigration history (Smith and Moore 2000).

I will use the quantitative data to test the effects of family socioeconomic status on college graduation. Both quantitative and interview data are employed to understand the cultural explanations for the college graduation rates of immigrant and native Blacks. Mixed methods are also used to address the effect of intellectual integration on college persistence. The qualitative data is cautiously used to address the overrepresentation of immigrant Blacks at UC campuses. I present the qualitative data to show that Black college students understand this disparity in terms of perceived cultural differences between immigrant and native Blacks. The respondents also discuss the outcomes of their Black childhood and high school contemporaries, providing a biased, yet illuminating glimpse into the different post-secondary paths of young Black people.

RESULTS FROM THE STATISTICAL DATA

At a 2004 Harvard reunion for Black students, Lani Guinier, a Harvard law professor, and Henry Louis Gates Jr., a professor in the African and African-American studies department, made an observation that was considered surprising, or at least newsworthy, at the time: that immigrant Blacks and their children make up the majority of Harvard alumni (Rimer and Arenson 2004). Since that time, an empirical study showed that immigrant Blacks are overrepresented in elite colleges (Massey, et al. 2007); while other studies have found the same in post-secondary institutions in general (Bennett and Lutz 2009, Glick and White 2004, Rong and Brown 2001, Hagy and Staniec 2002).

Considering the proportion of college-aged immigrant Blacks in California, they are overrepresented within the Black population on UC campuses (Figure 6.1). Immigrant Blacks are only one-tenth of the college-aged Black population in California yet they are almost one-third of the UC student population. The data does not include applicants to the UC system, so it is not possible to determine the role socioeconomic status in college matriculation; however, previous empirical studies show the relationship between socioeconomic status and educational attainment (Kao and Thompson 2003). Given their overwhelming socioeconomic advantage (Dodoo 1997, Djamba 1999), it is not surprising that immigrant Blacks are overrepresented among Black college students.

Figure 6.1: Immigrant and Native Blacks in California and UC system

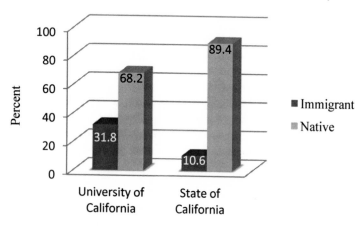

State of California, Department of Finance (2009), U.S. Census Bureau 2000
College-aged, 18-25 year old, Blacks in California (n = 249,728). UC system (n = 876)

Socioeconomic status of Black UC students
The statistical data from the University of California Undergraduate Experience Survey (UCUES) shows that immigrant Black UC students' fathers follow the pattern of parental educational attainment for UC students of all ethnicities (Figure 2.6). While fathers of native Black students have high levels of education, immigrant Black fathers are more likely to have a bachelor's degree or an advanced degree (Figures 6.2). Similar to results found by Massey, et al. (2007), household income is statistically equal in the two groups (figure not shown). At least in terms of paternal educational attainment, immigrant Black students are more likely than native Black students to have college-educated role models. I examine paternal education by campus selectivity to ascertain the distribution in those populations.

Figure 6.2: Father's education by immigrant generation, Black UC students (n = 598)

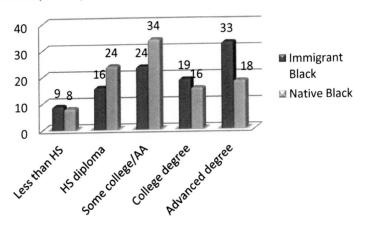

Chi-square significant at the 0.001 level

Differences in socioeconomic status by immigrant generation differ by campus selectivity. At the flagship and competitive campuses, there is no difference in immigrant versus native Black students' father's education. Paternal education differs by immigrant generation for Black students at less competitive campuses. Fathers of immigrant Black students are more almost three times more likely to have an advanced degree (Figure 6.3). More than 50% of immigrant Black fathers have at least a bachelor's degree, compared to about 27% of native Blacks. In this case, there is a clear advantage for immigrant Black students in terms of father's education.

Empirical research underscores the importance of parental education to Black children's college matriculation (Glick and White 2004, Hagy and Staniec 2002). Bennett and Lutz (2009) are able to account for the overrepresentation of immigrant Blacks versus native Blacks in college by controlling for socioeconomic status and other background factors. Thus, it will be important to control for socioeconomic status in statistical models predicting college graduation.

Figure 6.3: Father's education by immigrant generation – Black students at less competitive campuses (n =179)

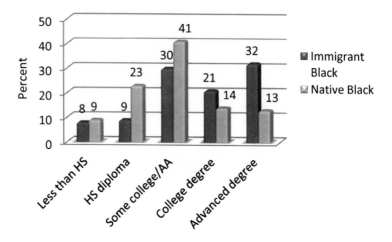

Chi-square significant at the 0.01 level

Intellectual integration
I operationalize Tinto's concept of intellectual integration using the variable "I feel I belong at this campus." In Chapter 3, I used this belonging variable to understand ethnic differences in college student experience. That analysis showed that Black students have a different, less satisfactory, college experience than students of other ethnicities.

As described in Chapter 3, intellectual integration occurs when a student feels her values align with the values of other members of the university (students, faculty, and staff). In Chapter 5, I explored Black students' perceptions of discrimination on campus. If Black students perceive that others within the university are racially prejudiced, this can negatively impact their intellectual integration. Similarly, Black students may discount academic assessments and devalue academic success if they feel they are being judged based on their race (Schmader, Major, and Gramzow 2001).

In Chapter 3, I presented a regression predicting sense of belonging for the Black student population. As mentioned earlier, Black students are less likely than students of other ethnicities to feel they belong at their campus. Black students' feelings of belonging did not differ significantly by immigrant generation. In the present chapter, I present a regression model predicting sense of belonging. There are important differences between the model in the Chapter 3 and the present model. In the previous model, diversity was tested, whereas in the present model, campus selectivity is used to model institutional differences. The present model also expands upon the previous regression by including all ethnicities.

Table 6.1 contains the odds ratios for the binary logistic regression predicting the variable belonging for students of all ethnicities at all UC campuses. Immigrant and second-generation immigrant students are less likely than native students to have a sense of belonging. This difference by immigrant generation does not hold for Black students (Table 3.3). Not surprisingly, college grade point average is positively related to intellectual integration. However, the causality of this relationship could be reversed or mutually reinforcing.

Black students are less likely than White students to have a sense of belonging on campus (Table 6.1). Also, belonging differs by institution. Students at flagship campuses versus students at less competitive campuses are more likely to feel they belong (Table 6.1, Model 3). The odds ratio of the interaction terms show much larger the odds ratio for an ethnic group would at flagship or competitive campuses compared to less competitive campuses. For example, the interaction term Black*Flagship shows that Black students are significantly more likely to have a sense of belonging at flagship and competitive campuses, versus less competitive campuses (Table 6.1,

Table 6.1: Binary logistic regression predicting "I feel like I belong at this campus," all UC students

Predictor Variable	Model 1 Exp(B)		Model 2 Exp(B)		Model 3 Exp(B)		Model 4 Exp(B)	
Background characteristics								
Immigrant or second-generation	0.785	***	0.788	***	0.780	***	0.781	***
Female	1.084	*	1.061		1.028		1.027	
Black	0.429	***	0.457	***	0.455	***	0.927	
Chicano/Latino	0.942		0.968		0.978		1.267	*
Asian	0.775	***	0.771	***	0.786	***	0.866	
White	ref		ref		ref		ref	
Mother's education	1.049	*	1.047	*	1.047	*	1.048	*
Father's education	1.048	**	1.040	**	1.036	*	1.036	
Parents' income	1.018		1.021		1.023		1.022	
High school factors								
High school grade point average			1.325	***	1.111	***	1.099	
SAT I score			1.000		1.000	**	1.000	**

Table 6.1: Binary logistic regression predicting "I feel like I belong at this campus," all UC students (Continued)

Predictor Variable	Model 1 Exp(B)		Model 2 Exp(B)		Model 3 Exp(B)		Model 4 Exp(B)	
College factors								
College grade point average					1.313	***	1.319	***
Campus selectivity								
Flagships					1.191	**	1.319	***
Competitive					1.075		1.256	**
Less competitive					ref		ref	
Interactions ethnicity*campus								
Black*Flagships							0.327	***
Black*Competitive							0.381	**
Chicano/Latino*Flagships							0.708	*
Chicano/Latino*Competitive							0.721	**
Asian*Flagships							0.972	
Asian*Competitive							0.836	
Constant	1.155		0.420	*	0.494	**	0.468	***
Number of cases	17,835		17,835		17,835		17,835	
Nagelkerke R^2	0.028		0.031		0.035		0.038	

*significant at the 0.05 level, **significant at the 0.01 level, ***significant at the 0.001 level
The notation "ref" is for the reference category of a set of variables.

Model 4). Results in Chapter 3 also show institutional effects on Black students' sense of belonging. To summarize, Black students at more ethnically diverse schools are more likely to feel they belong. Without describing the particular situation at each campus, these results demonstrate the importance of the institutional milieu in Black students' intellectual integration on campus. University administrators, student services, course selection, funding for student groups, and many other institution-level factors inform Black students' feelings of belonging.

Graduation by ethnicity and immigrant generation
First I examined the continued enrollment and graduation rates of UC students by ethnicity and immigrant generation. For Blacks, Chicano/Latinos, and Whites, there was no difference in graduation rate by immigrant generation (Figure 6.7). Native Asian students were more likely than immigrant Asian students to graduate (Chi-square significant at the 0.01 level).

I also examined graduation rates by campus selectivity, with categories based on the average high school grade point average and SAT I score of incoming freshmen. As with the overall UC population, graduation rates for immigrants and natives were statistically equal for Blacks, Chicano/Latinos, and Whites. For Asians at the flagship campuses and the less selective campuses, there was no difference in graduation rate by family immigration history. Only at the competitive campuses did native Asian students have a higher graduation rate than immigrant Asian students (Chi-square significant at the 0.01 level).

Although regression analysis implies a unidirectional causation, the relationship between intellectual integration and college academic performance is likely bi-directional. If a student feels she belongs on campus, she may feel secure about to participating in class and feel motivated to study. Doing well in class may enhance her sense of belonging. In the following models, I am testing the presence and significance of the relationship between intellectual integration and college academic performance, rather than a causal relationship.

To test the relationship of intellectual integration on graduation, I ran five binary logistic regression analyses: one for all UC students and one for each ethnicity. For each analysis, the first model has several background variables: immigrant generation, sex, mother's education, father's education, and parents' income. The second model adds high school performance variables. The third model has institutional effects, measured by campus selectivity. Lastly, the intellectual integration variable, "I feel I belong at this campus" is added.

Figure 6.4: Persistence by ethnicity and immigrant generation

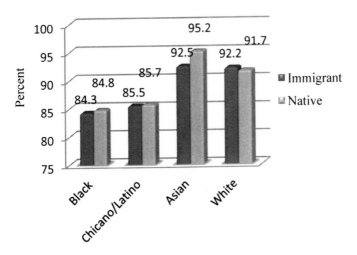

*Chi-square significant at the 0.01 level
Black, n = 815; Chicano/Latino, n = 4,488; Asian, n = 13,727; White, n = 14,964

Table 6.2 presents the odds ratios for the binary logistic regression on graduation for all UC students. Controlling for background characteristics, high school performance, and campus selectivity, Black and Chicano/Latino students are less likely than White students to graduate, while Asian students are more likely (Table 6.2, Model 3). The Black-White graduation gap is less pronounced and less significant when intellectual integration is taken into account (Table 6.2, Model 4). Female students are 1.2 times more likely to graduate (Table 6.2, Models 4), as predicted by the literature (Grant and Rong 1999, Kleinfeld 1999). Also in line with empirical studies (for example, Gansemer-Topf and Schuh 2006) is the finding that students at less selective schools are less likely to graduate (Table 6.2, Model 3).

Table 6.2: Intellectual integration correlates of continued enrollment or graduation, all UC students

Predictor Variable	Model 1 Exp(B)		Model 2 Exp(B)		Model 3 Exp(B)		Model 4 Exp(B)	
Background characteristics								
Immigrant or second-generation	1.012		1.057		1.036		1.063	
Native	ref		ref		ref		ref	
Female	1.328	***	1.238	***	1.228	***	1.237	***
Male	ref		ref		ref		ref	
Black	0.456	***	0.697	*	0.664	**	0.732	*
Chicano/Latino	0.620	***	0.760	**	0.746	**	0.743	***
Asian	1.211	*	1.226	*	1.224	*	1.273	***
White	ref		ref		ref		ref	
Mother's education	0.990		.984		0.992		0.984	
Father's education	1.110	***	1.069	*	1.074	*	1.073	*
Parents' income	1.045		1.043		1.056		1.053	
High school factors								
High school grade point average			4.109	***	3.346	***	3.349	***
SAT I score			1.000	*	1.000		1.000	

Table 6.2: Intellectual integration correlates of continued enrollment or graduation, all UC students (Continued)

Predictor Variable	Model 1 Exp(B)		Model 2 Exp(B)		Model 3 Exp(B)		Model 4 Exp(B)	
Campus selectivity								
Flagships					1.690	***	1.677	***
Competitive					1.394	***	1.393	***
Less competitive					ref		1.734	***
Intellectual integration variable								
"I feel I belong at this campus"				***			1.734	***
Constant	5.253	***	0.017	***	0.039	***	0.030	***
Number of cases	20,519		16,748		16,748		16,580	
Nagelkerke R^2	0.024		0.084		0.088		0.101	

*significant at the 0.05 level, **significant at the 0.01 level, ***significant at the 0.001 level
The notation "ref" is for the reference category of a set of variables.

In order to show the correlates of graduation for each ethnicity, I present separate regression models for each population. In the case of intellectual integration, the variable is a *correlate* of graduation, rather than a *predictor* of graduation, since intellectual integration and academic achievement affect each other. In Chapters 4 and 5, there are other models predicting graduation with correlates relevant to those respective chapters. The models in the current chapter test the significance of intellectual integration on graduation. As with the full UC population, the models restricted to separate ethnicities each show a significant positive relationship with intellectual integration.

In the model restricted to Black students, a sense of belonging on campus is significantly correlated with graduation (Table 6.3, Model 4). Those Black students who agree with the belonging statement are 2.4 times more likely to graduate. Along with academic performance in high school, intellectual integration is the only significant predictor of graduation in the model for Black students (Table 6.3, Model 4). None of the measures of socioeconomic status (mother's education, father's education, and parents' income) is significantly related to graduation (Table 6.3, Model 1).

Table 6.4 presents the odds ratios for the Chicano/Latino population. These findings are similar to those of Black students: high school grade point average and belonging significantly predict graduation (Table 6.4, Model 4). In addition, students at less competitive school are less likely to graduate than students at the flagship campuses (Table 6.4, Model 3).

In the model restricted to Asian students, intellectual integration positively and significantly affects graduation (Table 6.5, Model 4). Similar to the model for Chicano/Latino students, campus selectivity is important for Asian students' probability of graduation. Asian students at flagship campuses are more likely to graduate than Asian students at competitive and less competitive schools (Table 6.5, Model 3). High school academic performance is also significantly related to graduation for Asians. Unlike students of other ethnicities, gender affects graduation: female Asian students are 1.4 times more likely to graduate than their male counterparts (Table 6.5, Model 4).

In the model for White students, the importance of intellectual integration is again evident. White students who feel they belong on campus are 2.3 times more likely to graduate (Table 6.6, Model 4). As

Table 6.3: Intellectual integration correlates of continued enrollment or graduation, Black students

Predictor Variable	Model 1 Exp(B)	Model 2 Exp(B)		Model 3 Exp(B)		Model 4a Exp(B)	
Background characteristics							
Immigrant or second-generation	0.957	0.790		0.761		0.738	
Native	ref	ref		ref		ref	
Female	0.922	0.825		0.857		0.897	
Male	ref	ref		ref		ref	
Mother's education	1.201	1.345		1.342		1.348	
Father's education	0.849	0.771		0.774		0.776	
Parents' income	1.037	1.034		1.048		1.013	
High school factors							
High school grade point average		3.221	**	3.276	**	3.120	**
SAT I score		1.000		1.000		1.000	
Campus selectivity							
Flagships				0.975		1.235	
Competitive				1.510		1.833	
Less competitive				ref		ref	

Table 6.3: Intellectual integration correlates of continued enrollment or graduation, Black students (Continued)

Predictor Variable	Model 1 Exp(B)		Model 2 Exp(B)		Model 3 Exp(B)		Model 4a Exp(B)	
Intellectual integration variable								
"I feel I belong at this campus"							2.405	**
Constant	4.654			***			0.075	
Number of cases	422		0.070		0.061		345	
Nagelkerke R^2	0.011		347		347		0.111	
			0.074		0.083			

*significant at the 0.05 level, **significant at the 0.01 level, ***significant at the 0.001 level

The notation "ref" is for the reference category of a set of variables.

Table 6.4: Intellectual integration correlates of continued enrollment or graduation, Chicano/Latino students

Predictor Variable	Model 1 Exp(B)	Model 2 Exp(B)		Model 3 Exp(B)		Model 4a Exp(B)	
Background characteristics							
Immigrant or second-generation	1.077	1.094		1.069		1.063	
Native	ref	ref		ref		ref	
Female	1.211	1.171		1.158		1.191	
Male	ref	ref		ref		ref	
Mother's education	1.027	1.009		1.022		1.001	
Father's education	1.056	1.010		1.012		1.016	
Parents' income	1.055	1.031		1.047		1.045	
High school factors							
High school grade point average		3.685	***	3.156	***	3.159	***
SAT I score		1.000		1.000		1.000	
Campus selectivity							
Flagships				1.491	*	1.513	*
Competitive				1.245		1.270	
Less competitive				ref		ref	

Table 6.4: Intellectual integration correlates of continued enrollment or graduation, Chicano/Latino students (Continued)

Predictor Variable	Model 1 Exp(B)		Model 2 Exp(B)		Model 3 Exp(B)		Model 4a Exp(B)	
Intellectual integration variable								
"I feel I belong at this campus"							1.596	***
Constant	3.902	***	0.022	***	0.041	***	0.031	***
Number of cases	2763		2187		2187		2158	
Nagelkerke R²	0.005		0.065		0.068		0.080	

*significant at the 0.05 level, **significant at the 0.01 level, ***significant at the 0.001 level
The notation "ref" is for the reference category of a set of variables.

Table 6.5: Intellectual integration correlates of continued enrollment or graduation, Asian students

Predictor Variable	Model 1 Exp(B)		Model 2 Exp(B)		Model 3 Exp(B)		Model 4 Exp(B)	
Background characteristics								
Immigrant or second-generation	0.606	*	0.673		0.657		0.676	
Native	ref		ref		ref		ref	
Female	1.456	***	1.413	***	1.395	***	1.397	***
Male	ref		ref		ref		ref	
Mother's education	.963		.937		0.944		0.952	
Father's education	1.116	*	1.059		1.056		1.051	
Parents' income	1.056		1.067		1.086		1.078	
High school factors								
High school grade point average			3.973	***	3.169	***	3.167	***
SAT I score			1.001	*	1.000		1.000	

Table 6.5: Intellectual integration correlates of continued enrollment or graduation, Asian students (Continued)

Predictor Variable	Model 1 Exp(B)		Model 2 Exp(B)		Model 3 Exp(B)		Model 4 Exp(B)	
Campus selectivity								
Flagships					ref		ref	
Competitive					0.653	**	0.663	**
Less competitive					0.593	**	0.611	**
Intellectual integration								
"I feel I belong at this campus"							1.241	*
Constant	11.904	***	0.025	***	0.127	**	0.108	**
Number of cases	8324		7039		7039		6959	
Nagelkerke R^2	0.012		0.073		0.077		0.079	

*significant at the 0.05 level, **significant at the 0.01 level, ***significant at the 0.001 level
The notation "ref" is for the reference category of a set of variables.

Table 6.6: Intellectual integration correlates of continued enrollment or graduation, White students

Predictor Variable	Model 1 Exp(B)		Model 2 Exp(B)		Model 3 Exp(B)		Model 4 Exp(B)	
Background characteristics								
Immigrant or second-generation	1.109		1.190		1.178		1.252	*
Native	ref		ref		ref			
Female	1.323	***	1.163		1.159		1.155	
Male	ref		ref					
Mother's education	0.967		0.985		0.991		0.977	
Father's education	1.182	***	1.177	***	1.179	**	1.177	**
Parents' income	1.029		1.026		1.027		1.021	
High school factors								
High school grade point average			4.606	***	3.644	***	3.757	***
SAT I score			1.000		1.000		1.000	

Table 6.6: Intellectual integration correlates of continued enrollment or graduation, White students (Continued)

Predictor Variable	Model 1 Exp(B)		Model 2 Exp(B)		Model 3 Exp(B)		Model 4 Exp(B)	
Campus selectivity								
Flagships					ref		ref	
Competitive					0.970		0.987	
Less competitive					0.547	***	0.569	***
Intellectual integration								
"I feel I belong at this campus"							2.317	***
Constant	5.784	***	0.011	***	0.025	***	0.029	***
Number of cases	9010		7175		7150		7118	
Nagelkerke R^2	0.009		0.072		0.164		0.111	

*significant at the 0.05 level, **significant at the 0.01 level, ***significant at the 0.001 level
The notation "ref" is for the reference category of a set of variables.

with Chicano/Latino and Asian students, attending a less competitive school has a negative effect on graduation for White students (Table 6.6, Model 3). Also similar to the other ethnicities, high school grade point average is correlated with graduation (Table 6.6, Model 2). Notable predictors for White students' graduation rates are socioeconomic status, as measured by father's education (Table 6.6, Model 1) and family immigration history, with immigrant Whites 1.3 times more likely to graduate than native Whites (Table 6.6, Model 4).

Summary of statistical analyses
Although there were differences in the parental education levels of immigrant versus native Blacks, socioeconomic status variables were not significant predictors of Black student graduation. There is no difference in the graduation rates of immigrant versus native Blacks across the UC system or by campus selectivity. Additionally, family immigration history is not a significant predictor of graduation in the binary logistic regression model for Black students. These findings resonate with the thesis of a Black college experience that transcends immigrant generation.

Black students were much less likely than White students to have a sense of belonging on campus, controlling for background variables. This finding builds upon the observation in Chapter 3 that intellectual integration is less likely among Black versus non-Black students (Figure 3.2). Taken together, they point to a unique Black experience on campus.

Intellectual integration was significantly related to Black student graduation. Those Black students who felt they belonged on campus were more likely to graduate. This relationship is likely cyclical – with successful students being more likely to be intellectually integrated as well as intellectually integrated students being more likely to do well in class. Intellectual integration accounts for some of the Black-White college graduation gap. Intellectual integration is beneficial to academic outcomes across ethnic groups. For the model including all ethnicities, as well as the models for each ethnicity, the belonging variable is a significant, positive predictor of graduation. Beyond the intellectual integration variable, the models for each ethnicity were very different from each other. This underscores the need for theories of college persistence that either vary by ethnicity or can capture the crucial factors for each ethnicity.

Intellectual integration varied by campus, with stronger feelings of belonging at more selective schools. In Chapter 4, I offered larger endowments as an explanation for greater social integration at flagship campuses. This explanation is reasonable in this situation as well. Endowments are used to fund undergraduate scholarships. UC tuition is set by the UC Office of the President and is the same at each campus. If a school can offer greater financial aid, their students may feel more valued and have a stronger sense of intellectual integration into the campus.

RESULTS FROM THE QUALITATIVE DATA

The existing literature shows that a substantial portion of the disparity in college matriculation immigrant and native Blacks can be explained by social class (Hagy and Staniec 2002, Glick and White 2004, Bennett and Lutz 2009). There has been much scholarly interest in cultural explanations; however, empirical quantitative tests are mixed. After controlling for socioeconomic status, some researchers find an immigrant advantage in educational attainment (Hagy and Staniec 2002, Glick and White 2004), while others do not (Bennett and Lutz 2009). Clearly parental income and education have a large impact on children's education, but is that the whole story? Is there an immigrant effect beyond the high levels of parental education among immigrant Blacks?

The qualitative data collected for this study are used to explore the cultural narratives that Black students hold regarding the differences between and similarities among immigrant and native Blacks, especially as they pertain to academic achievement. I focus on the concepts of dual frame of reference (Ogbu 1991), and social capital of the family, co-ethnic community, and peers (Portes and Zhou 1993). I explore the reasons that the interviewees give for the overrepresentation of immigrant Blacks relative to native Blacks in college. This analysis is not meant to validate cultural explanations, but simply to present the narratives that Black college students have about the disproportions within the Black college-going population.

Lastly, I look Black students' feelings of belonging in the institution. Previous empirical work on Black students in predominantly White institutions has found that Black students band together, regardless of differences in background (Willie 2003, Smith and Moore 2000). I found this camaraderie was also true for immigrant and native Black students, as I reported Chapter 4. In the present analysis, I focus on the way Black students talk about their place within the university, paying special attention to potential differences by family immigration history. The interview data are used to examine Black students' sense of belonging on campus, linking the statistical analysis of intellectual integration with the interview findings. This qualitative analysis is a deeper look into the concept of intellectual integration, which was a significant predictor of Black students' likelihood of graduation, in the regression model presented in an earlier section of this chapter (Table 6.3, Model 4).

More immigrant Blacks than native Blacks in college

The respondents in this present study, immigrant and native, commented on the disproportionate numbers of immigrant Blacks on campus. Adenike, a Nigerian American student, talked about her observations about immigrant and native Black young people's paths:

> In colleges and universities, people who represent the Black community are African people these days. If you see a Black man on campus, ask him if he's Black or if he's African. He'll most likely tell you his parents are from Africa. You'll find more African people or Nigerian people in school than on the streets. I don't know any Nigerian rappers, but there's a lot of Black rappers. (Adenike, Nigerian American, first-year student)

Adenike's parents were professionals who owned their home. She described her neighborhood and schools as "very rich," yet native Black young men she knew mostly did not go on to college. With one exception, a young man who joined the Army, all the young Nigerian men she knows are in college.

Talking about her particular university, a young native Black woman said, "A lot of the kids here, their parents are from Africa.

There are very few whose parents were born here." (Raven, native Black female, first-year student) Raven's father has a blue-collar job, and she described her mother's occupation as homemaker. They rent their home. When I asked about native Black men she grew up with, Raven told me stories of young fatherhood and minimum wage jobs.

Immigrant and native Black respondents commented on the overrepresentation of immigrant Blacks in the Black student community. Empirical studies demonstrate that socioeconomic status explains much (or all) of this disparity (Bennett and Lutz 2009, Hagy and Staniec 2002, Glick and White 2004). However, an additional explanation that arises from the interviews is cultural: immigrant Blacks have the optimistic worldview and the social capital to motivate them academically. I examine the qualitative data for Black college students' understanding of a cultural immigrant advantage.

Dual frame of reference: Immigrant Blacks
Immigrant Black respondents in this study had a positive dual frame of reference with regard to educational opportunities in the U.S. versus in their home countries. Viewing the U.S. educational system through the lens of their immigrant background, it is an amazing opportunity. As the respondents explain, the educational system and occupational structure in their home countries are not as open as they are in the U.S. Perhaps school is not available to everyone or is not subsidized by the government. Perhaps career opportunities are limited because of the economy of the country. Immigrants have a positive dual frame of reference, comparing their situation in the U.S. with the situation in their home country and finding that life in the U.S. offers hope for educational and economic advancement. This viewpoint was evident in my interviews.

Bin, who is Ethiopian and Filipino, described the educational and economic situation in his father's home country:

> They [first-generation Ethiopians] view academics a lot more importantly. They have higher standards. They saw what happened back at home. Not everyone has the opportunity to go to school and once you graduate, the jobs are, there's barely any jobs. So in order to just find a job and have an opportunity, they're very thankful so they work very hard.

(Bin, U.S.-born Ethiopian and Filipino male, first-year student)

Despite a bachelor's degree in Business from a university in Ethiopia, Bin's father was a truck driver in his home country. He is a truck driver in the U.S. as well.

Robel, an Eritrean respondent whose parents owned a custodial business in the U.S., explained his parents' point of view:

> You grew up there and seen the contrast, you know what you're coming from. A lot of people who may be African American who grow up here don't have that same drive because they haven't come from the same sort of poverty. My parents came from poverty beyond any poverty here. To them, when they see here there are so many opportunities... I see my dad, the way he views things here, he's very optimistic. He tries to see things as opportunities, not as obstacles. He's trying to get what he wants to get, so everything is, 'How can I make this to my benefit?' He tries to make it a positive. People here, maybe they're just numb to it. I notice that. (Robel, Eritrean male, immigrated to the U.S. when two years old, fourth-year student)

Robel's parents each completed the equivalent of a high school diploma in Eritrea. His observation that his father sees opportunities rather than obstacles echoes Ogbu's (1991) assertion that, because of their positive dual frame of reference, immigrant minorities are less likely than involuntary minorities to perceive discrimination as a barrier to success.

Oladapo was born in the U.S. and his father sent him to Nigeria when he was young so he would know his cultural background. He returned to the U.S. when he was 13 years old. He explained his Nigerian friends' situations:

> We know the benefits of an education. In Nigeria, most people don't have the opportunity to go to school, get an education, get a well-paying job. So we know what an education can do, it can really transform your life. So if you have that

opportunity, don't take it for granted. Most people try to go overseas because the opportunities are very limited in Nigeria. For an undergraduate degree, here it takes four years, just like that. Over there, it might take six years, seven years. They have this period of strike where teachers refuse to teach because they're not being paid and schools will close down for several months, you're just at home, not going to school. It's very frustrating. My mates in Nigeria, I'm graduating now, but they're probably not graduating yet. They probably have another two more years to complete their undergraduate degree... So when you have an opportunity like this, you grab onto it for dear life. (Oladapo, Nigerian male, fourth-year student)

His parents both have bachelor's degrees from California State Universities: his father in Engineering and his mother in Business.

Respondents link this positive dual frame of reference to matriculation to college. Seeing the difference in educational opportunities in their home countries and in the U.S., immigrant Blacks feel a responsibility and a familial expectation to go to college. I asked the respondents about their Black friends growing up, and where those friends are now. The answers of the Nigerian respondents stood out from the rest. Each of the 12 interviewees who identify as Nigerian or Nigerian American said that the vast majority of their Nigerian friends were in college. A few mentioned Nigerian friends who were not in college, but these non-college-goers were clearly exceptions to the rule. For the other eight immigrant Black respondents (not Nigerian), there was more variation in the outcomes of their co-ethnic friends. The other immigrant Black respondents talked about friends in college, but also had friends who were working minimum-wage jobs, not working, or involved in criminal activity.

I asked immigrant Black respondents about the co-ethnic friends they had growing up, and where they were today. The typical answer from a Nigerian respondent is represented by Eniola's answer, that her co-ethnic friends are virtually all in college:

I would put a 100% rate on that if I didn't know one boy who didn't do that. He's an outlier, so I can excuse him. It's basically 100%. Every Nigerian I've encountered, it's high school, it's college, it's future, it's being successful in this country so you can sustain yourself. *We're not from here, back home we didn't have the same opportunities.* [emphasis added] (Eniola, Nigerian American female, first-year student)

Eniola's parents have graduate degrees and professional careers. There is clearly a cultural narrative about why immigrant Blacks go to college. The immigrant Black respondents ascribe a positive dual frame of reference to their parents and appear to have adopted it themselves.

Dual frame of reference: Native Blacks

Some native Black respondents exhibit a negative dual frame of reference in terms of their pre-college opportunities vis-à-vis more economically-advantaged groups in the U.S. They talked about the socioeconomic disadvantage around them when they were growing up. As college students, they felt they were the exception among their peer group growing up. Ten of the 19 native Black interviewees said some of the native Black children they knew growing up were now working minimum-wage jobs. It is notable that among the 19 native Black respondents, 13 mention *street life* as one of the outcomes of their native Black friends. The idea of street life was brought up by both immigrant and native Blacks to describe people who were: in prison, having children before they were ready, selling drugs, or involved in gangs.

James told me about his friends from home:

They're not in college, I'll tell you that. Most of them are working what I call a common job. Other than that, most of them are breaking the law pretty much. I went to a low-budget middle school, four people to a textbook. It was bad, really bad... I believe that the average African American male in America does not believe they're going to live past 18. That's a fact. A lot of people in my old neighborhood feel like that. I went to one of my old friend's 18th birthday and he said, 'Man, I didn't think I was going to live this long.' (James, native Black male)

He cited low-resource schools as part of the reason his contemporaries work minimum-wage jobs or engage in illegal activities. Although his mother had a modest income and he had no contact with his father, James attended a selective, private high school on scholarship. He excelled academically and said he chose his university over Harvard, Princeton, and University of Michigan. He talked about his choice not to engage in street life:

> As I grew older and older, I saw it's [street life] bad but also another reason, it's a waste of money. Now I'm really not going to do it... A lot of people find the fast life as *the only way* to better their situation, although hundreds and hundreds of people have tried it and like maybe one has succeeded. I'm a man of numbers. That's why I didn't go to a historically Black college. The number of people who come from a historically Black college who become millionaires is significantly lower than the people coming out of [his college]. [emphasis added] (James)

He didn't want to engage in street life, which was one of the few options open to him, and the "only way" for many around him. Instead, he decided college, a prestigious college, was the most efficacious way to succeed in life.

Ayana said that her father is an unemployed regional transit bus driver and her mother is a homemaker. She said that the native Black males she knew growing up have disparate trajectories:

> Some are in jail. A few are going to school. Quite a few are in jail and then some passed, a couple passed away, they were killed. Most of them are either going to school or just working normal jobs, minimum wage-type jobs. (Ayana, native Black female)

She said of the Black females:

> More of them [girls] are working, probably not in school. More of them are working. A lot of the girls I grew up with

have kids now. I don't know very much about the fathers. I don't know if the fathers are around very much. (Ayana)

From her description most of her childhood peers have already joined the workforce and "quite a few" are in prison.

Similarly, Robert described the road to college as one that not many of his peers survived:

> It's just a weeding out system where not many African American males get focused and survive through high school and get to college and do what they need to do... There are two different kinds of people in this world, there are people who go to work and get paid and work, work, work, work, work, work, work, work, work, all the way through their lives then when they're seventy, they just chill. And then there are people who are in college and they just really work, really work, really work for four straight years. And after the four years are over, you're like 23 or 24 and you just chill. So I guess that's the type of mindset that we [he and his high school friends] had. (Robert, native Black male)

He lived primarily with his mother, who had an Associate's degree and was a medical technician. According to Robert, not getting "weeded out," gives him the opportunity to have a white-collar job where he can "just chill" versus a blue-collar job that is constant work until you retire.

Bradley said he considered not finishing college then reconsidered:

> I've thought about it, but then I think about the neighborhood I grew up in or what would happen to me if I couldn't finish school. I grew up in the inner city... That's why, for me, failure is not an option because of the life, what I would be subject to if I didn't graduate from school... I wouldn't have the opportunity to do anything. I would have to live in a neighborhood with violence, poor education. I wouldn't be able to help my kids have opportunities. (Bradley, native Black male)

Bradley's parents both have high school diplomas. His father is unemployed and his mother has a blue-collar job. Native Black college students feel they've navigated a treacherous road to college. They view education as the pathway to success, but one that accommodates only a few hard-working, lucky ones. And even those few who have made it to college do not feel far from the street life they described.

> Brandi's native Black male friends were in college:
> Some of my male cousins are in jail for doing the activities that they do. That's what I think about when I think of [her three Black male friends who *are* in college]. I'm just happy that they're not incarcerated.

Brandi's parents both work, earning about $100,000 per year. She attended a private, Catholic high school. It is telling that she views prison as the alternative to college for these young men. Other qualitative research echoes these respondents' belief that young Black men are one step away from incarceration (Smith and Fleming 2006).

> Maurice bluntly explained:
> Most of my friends that I go back to see are either at a community college or a state school. I didn't really hang out with anybody who wasn't going anywhere.

His parents had professional jobs and owned their home. He grew up in a middle-class neighborhood and went to a good public high school. However, many native Black kids Maurice knew growing up were more focused on what he called "ghetto culture" than on school. He felt the need to surround himself with academically-motivated friends. Those native Blacks he did not associate with were enamored of "the nice clothes, the brand-name clothes, the new shoes every week or so, and then this whole image of being tough and with a clique." Although Maurice presents "ghetto culture" and academic ambition as mutually exclusive, recent research questions this relationship (Warikoo 2011).

The native Black respondents ascribe a negative dual frame of reference to their native Black peers. When asked about their native Black peers from childhood and high school, many respondents described trajectories much different from their own: teenage parents, prison, minimum-wage jobs, and untimely deaths. The interviewees were the exceptions, and they knew it.

Family social capital

In many ways, parental education affects the academic attainment of children (Kao and Thompson 2003). Segmented assimilation theory focuses on the benefits of the immigrant family in motivating second-generation immigrant children in school. I found overwhelming support for this in the interview data. Every one of the 20 immigrant Black respondents said their parents strongly encouraged them to go to and graduate from college.

I also found that native Black college students came from academically-oriented families. There was more variation in the native Black group: 14 of the 19 respondents said their parents encouraged them to go to and graduate from college. Four native Black respondents said their parents were not particularly supportive of their educational endeavors. And one native Black interviewee was encouraged by her mother to go to college, but encouraged by her father to get a job so she could be financially independent.

For the most part, native Black respondents said their parents pushed them in school. Kim was encouraged by both of her parents to go to college:

> My grandmother was a nurse, she went to college, that was my only grandparent that actually did [post] secondary education. It put a fire under my dad's butt who, in turn, lit a fire under my butt. Also, my mom's side, my grandmother didn't grow up with a lot, so that affected my mom. It wasn't a conversation in my household. I was going to college. I was finishing college. (Kim, native Black female)

Kim's parents had professional careers and owned their home. Their household income was over $180,000. There were no other post-secondary options for Kim. Because of her parents' expectations, she would go to college.

I asked Bradley why he was so set on finishing college. He replied,

Without education you don't have much opportunity... My parents, it was really my dad, he was real strict. I guess I always had potential, sixth and seventh grade, I goofed off, didn't take school seriously. With tough love, my dad he helped me get serious about school and then ever since eighth grade I've been an honor roll student. (Bradley, native Black male, parents' highest degree was a high school diploma)

These native Black respondents described parents who had high academic expectations for their children and were very involved in their schooling. For this population, strong family social capital is common.

Even when their parents did not go to school themselves, they held high expectations for their children. Ayana said her parents both went to college, but neither of them finished. When asked if she ever thought about dropping out of college, she replied,

No, my mom would have a fit... My mom always regretted not finishing [college]. And she was our teacher. She just always said, 'You guys have to go to college. You guys have to go to college. It's a great opportunity.' Even for just myself, what I feel I want to do. I know I'll need a college degree to do it. My parents, especially my mom, I want to do this for her. But also a large part is also for myself and what I feel my purpose is. (Ayana, native Black female)

Her family's household income was less than $40,000. Ayana had seven siblings, and her mother home-schooled each of them. Her five older siblings had graduated from college or were enrolled in college.

Although most parents of the native Black respondents insisted that their children go to college, a few were not so encouraging. Shanice said her mother was supportive, but her father encouraged her to get a job instead:

My father is anti-establishment and, 'You don't need to go to college to be smart. You need to just be on your own.' My mom's like, 'Go to school.' I just say to my dad, 'Well, I need to go to school because I can't do anything without a college

degree.' And he says, 'Yes, you can!' He was trying to make
me work when I was twelve and I'm like, 'Dude, I have to go
to school.' 'You could work too! I worked ever since I was
eight.' (Shanice, native Black female)

Shanice's mother was unemployed and her father was an entrepreneur.
Her parents never married. She lived with her mother on government
assistance. Of those whose parents did not encourage college-going,
native Black respondents said financial independence was their parents'
goal for them.

Imani, identified as Black, told me about her siblings' lives. She
has two older half-sisters who have high school diplomas. Her older
brother completed 11th grade. None of them went to college. Her
younger half-brother is 18 years old. He completed 10th grade and is
currently incarcerated. Imani told me that immigrant parents have high
expectations for their children. I asked her why she thinks that
immigrant Blacks see college as the only option after high school. She
replied,

> I always felt like, if my parents worked so hard to get me
> here... If my parents do all that, you better work your butt off
> in school. Your parents won't let you just hang around in the
> house, like African American kids. Like my older brother and
> my older sister, they both have kids and they're both not
> working. They just sit around the house because they have
> nothing to really strive for because they've had it handed to
> them more. (Imani, native Black female)

Her siblings live with her mother and her mother's husband. Her father
is incarcerated.

Jada's mother married a Nigerian man who had two children about
Jada's age. She and her mother moved in with her Nigerian step-father
and step-siblings, and she lived there for two years before going to
college. She witnessed the difference between native and immigrant
Blacks, in terms of post-secondary expectations, and she observed:

> For Africans, it's less acceptable to not be getting an
> education. If one of my African friends wasn't in school, I

think their parents would be extremely upset. They'd be like, 'What are you doing? Get on your grind. You need to get in school.' Even if they're doing bad stuff in the process of getting an education, they're going to be in school getting an education. If you're drinking and smoking and stuff like that, 'Ok, that's great, but get your work done.' But African Americans, at least the ones I know, if you just don't want to go to school, your parents are going to be mad, but they're not going to get on you for it. They're not going to be like, 'That's not acceptable.' It's not like that at all. (Jada, native Black female)

Both Jada's mother and father did not go beyond high school. Where education is stressed in African immigrant families, she sees financial independence as the goal that native Black parents have for their children:

I know my mom's ok as long as you're doing something. Even when my brother didn't want to go to college, or when he got in trouble, she was like, 'Then get a job, but you're not going to be living off of me.' I think that's the main thing, 'Don't live off of me.' If you're out of high school, that means you're grown. You can live with me, but you're going to get a job. I'm not going to be paying for your car and stuff like that. (Jada)

These native Black respondents are quick to compare their mothers with immigrant Black parents. They found immigrant Black parents to be much more focused on college for their children. Here again is the cultural narrative of difference between immigrant and native Black parents. However, the majority of the native Black college students whom I interviewed said their parents strongly encouraged them in school.

With the immigrant Black respondents, the parental expectation of college-going was ubiquitous. Itunu, whose father came to the U.S. on a student visa, said she has so much "courage and motivation" for college from her parents and extended family. She moved to an economically-depressed, crime-ridden area of Los Angeles when she was a teenager. She mused about what her life trajectory would be if she had *grown up* in that city:

> If I grew up in [inner city], I probably would have had a different... actually, no I wouldn't because my parents are still Nigerian, so they still have their culture. So, I think it's all about the family and what expectations they have for you. I have a lot of Nigerian American friends who grew up in the inner city, and they're right where I'm at: Stanford, Cal, UCLA. It's not about where you grew up, it's more about your family and who you're surrounding yourself with as you grow up. (Itunu, Nigerian female, immigrated to the U.S. at age four)

The narrative of cultural difference comes up again. She touched on the protective nature of the immigrant family; even in the inner city, nothing could alter her path to college because her family would be there to guide her.

Most immigrants from Nigeria are educated, wealthy, and motivated (Dodoo 1997); those traits helped them emigrate to the U.S. Itunu also spoke about the selectivity of the immigrant group:

> I feel like the expectations are higher because our parents are doctors, are lawyers, are engineers. You can't say, 'I can't do it.' They give you the reason you can do. The reason you're in America is because they did it. It's just more motivation, I guess. Our African parents had the motivation to get out... I feel that's their motivation and courage for us. 'If I did it, then you can do it more than I can' type of thing. (Itunu)

Her father was a lawyer who earned his JD in the U.S., and her mother was a social worker and has a bachelor's degree in Criminology.

Dele said his mother didn't let him go out socially when he was in high school. His favorite thing about college was the independence. Dele explained the importance his mother placed on education:

> Schooling was an imperative... If you didn't do well, you're like a criminal. That's probably not the analogy I wanted, but

it's like, if you're not doing well, then what are you doing?...
At least for my parents, life is just solely school at this point...
in terms of all these clubs I mentioned [that I'm in], my mom
is like, 'What are you doing in clubs? Is that what I'm paying
for? School!' (Dele, Nigerian American male)

Dele lives primarily with his mother; his parents were never married.
His mother is a medical professional and earns over $180,000. The
parental involvement described by Dele echoes Bradley, the native
Black interviewee who said his dad practiced "tough love" on him, to
motivate him in school.

Native and immigrant Black students in this study had parents who
expressed high educational expectations and who were involved in their
children's education. The concept of family social capital is often used
to describe an immigrant advantage (Bankston and Zhou 1995, Portes
and Rumbaut 2001). While academically-oriented family social capital
is ubiquitous for immigrant Black respondents, it is also very common
among native Black respondents.

Social capital of the co-ethnic community
Most immigrant Black respondents described growing up in closed
communities, in which sanctions for deviating from the norm were
harsh (Portes 1998, Coleman 1990). They felt tremendous social
pressure to go to and finish college. Many researchers have found that
second-generation immigrants benefit academically from this
community effect (Feliciano 2006, Portes and Rumbaut 2001, Bankston
and Zhou 1995).

Odalapo said that if he didn't go to college, other Nigerians in the
community would question him.

It would be very hard to face some of them. They'd
say, 'Oh, what are you doing? You're not in school?
What have you been doing all this time? Get your
butt in school.' We [Nigerians] have different
cultural values [than native Blacks]. We respect our
elders; they don't or I say they don't... Some of
them, their parents don't push them enough or they
don't have any interest in what they're doing in

school. Nigerian parents will always show interest in
what you're doing. Always worried about where
you're headed academically, always be on your case.
(Odalapo, Nigerian male)

As mentioned earlier, Odalapo's parents both have college degrees.
Their household income is about $100,000 per year. While explaining
the community pressure to go to college, he distinguished between
Nigerian parents and native Black parents. This is a common narrative
among the respondents, that immigrant Blacks, in general, are more
focused on education.

The immigrant Black respondents discussed college attendance
and graduation as compulsory part of belonging to their families and
their communities. Bin talked about his *one* Ethiopian friend who is
not at a four-year college:

He's 21 now, so he sort of feels he's an adult and he can do
whatever he wants. But there's definitely a pressure
especially because all the family and friends are so close, we
all talk about everyone. You can tell when they talk about
him, the mood is different. You can definitely sense it, in their
tone of voice. They try to avoid the fact, in front of his
parents, that he's not doing things. There's definitely
pressure. (Bin, Ethiopian and Filipino male, father is a truck
driver)

Immigrant Black students use words like "disgrace" and
"shameful" when talking about dropping out or choosing not to go to
college. Chika said the hardest thing about college for her are the
academic expectations that her family has for her. When I asked her if
she ever thought about not finishing college, she said,

I mean it wasn't really an option for me, but sometimes I felt
like, 'I can't do this.' It's something that I knew was not an
option, I need to finish college. I come from a society where
education is really highly valued. Everybody goes to college.
It's a shameful thing to me when I see kids here like, 'Yeah, I
don't want to go to college.' That's like Klingon to me.

Everybody goes to college! That's just the way it is. It's like breathing, you got to do it. (Chika, Nigerian female, mother and father have graduate degrees)

Her co-ethnic community has strong expectations of all young people in their social network. Nnenna, who, while growing up, spent almost every weekend at a family function or cultural gathering, feels the pressure of attending college:

I feel like I have to go to college where like maybe other people made the choice themselves. Because if I didn't go, I think I'd be a disgrace to my family. (Nnenna, Nigerian female, mother and father have graduate degrees)

Ezinne, whose father has a graduate degree and whose mother has a bachelor's degree, both from California State Universities, talked about the high prevalence of immigrant Blacks in top universities and attributed it to role models in the family and extended family:

It goes back to how we were raised. There were higher expectations of us. We're trying to meet those. Just the fact that you have an uncle or an aunty or a cousin that are up there [in terms of education]. It doesn't have to be your parents, it can be an aunty or uncle. (Ezinne, identified as Nigerian American)

Immigrant Black young people often belong to closed communities that value higher education. These findings resonate with segmented assimilation theory, that the co-ethnic community provides academic motivation for the second-generation immigrant.

Although segmented assimilation theory does not directly address native Blacks, the assumption is that poor native Blacks who live in economically-depressed areas will have an oppositional culture. As described earlier in this chapter, most native Black respondents had strong parental support for their educational endeavors. Although none of the native Black respondents discussed academic expectations or support from the larger native Black community, they did talk about forming academically-oriented peer groups.

Peer network social capital

Native Black respondents created peer networks with academically advantageous social capital. Since all of the interviewees are college students at a selective school, it is not surprising that their friends from childhood and high school are also in college. Supportive peer groups, coupled with the encouraging family structure described earlier in this chapter, may be the social capital necessary for native Blacks to succeed in the educational system.

Respondents talked about forming a peer group with others who were academically ambitious. Sherice, who is from an economically-depressed city in the San Francisco Bay Area, talked about her high school:

> I just kept within my close-knit network of friends. We were always the motivated ones. Even now, we're pretty much one of the few that don't have children, still doing good in school, out of high school into college. I try to stay within my network of friends. (Sherice, native Black female, mother was a civil servant and father was retired from a manual-labor job)

She went on to describe the great divide within the young Black people she grew up with:

> The top two percent of my class are all in four-year institutions and probably doing well. No one has children, just furthering their education. But everyone else I see... Most people have children or are dead or doing nothing with their lives. Some live at home with their parents. Some could be selling drugs. Some just wander around with nothing to do... Some are in jail. (Sherice)

She acknowledged the divergent paths and pointed out that only a small percentage goes on to college; the rest, "everyone else," appear stuck in a downward trajectory.

Robert, a native Black respondent who was presented earlier in this chapter, said he surrounded himself with the other high-achievers, and he and his friends were the ones left when all the others had been weeded out:

> They've just given up all hope. As the years pass on, tenth grade some of the students left the school, and by senior year all that was left was just those few individuals who are driven and those people are who my friends are. We made this decision early on just that there is no other option. It's either this or we live out on the streets and just not do anything. (Robert, native Black male)

Robert's parents were divorced and he lived with his mother who earned less than $40,000 per year. These young Black people surrounded themselves with like-minded peers. The social capital of their group of high-achieving friends helped them stay on the path to college. A key component of segmented assimilation theory is the co-ethnic community protecting young people from the negative influences of poor native minorities (Portes and Rumbaut 2001). The findings from this study suggest that some of these native minorities create their own protective communities, their own pockets of highly-motivated young people.

Intellectual integration: A sense of belonging
The preceding sections describe respondents' understandings of the disparity in the college-going rates of immigrant and native Blacks. I now look at the experiences of Blacks, once in college. One of the few predictors of Black student graduation is a sense of belonging (Table 3, Model 4). This variable is a measure of intellectual integration. The qualitative data illuminates the ways Black students, both immigrant and native, feel unsupported or excluded by their university.

In several ways, interviewees felt unsupported by agents or policies of the university. These experiences make it apparent to Black students that the values of the institution either discriminate against or are apathetic to the Black students. Intellectual integration, a critical factor in Tinto's model of student retention, hinges upon the student's perception that the university's values are similar to theirs. As described Chapter 5, immigrant and native Black respondents recounted experiences of discrimination from their classmates and instructors. I now present data that Black students, immigrant and native alike, feel they are not respected or supported on campus.

Jahzara, a native Black student, indicted the university for undermining Blacks' identity as students:

> Just the other day, we had Black Wednesday, where the Black students come together on campus... We were having a balloon toss. But the police came. I was so angry because it's like, 'Excuse me, we're students here too. This is our university. We're not doing anything to bother anyone.' The game maybe lasted for ten minutes, but you want to come outside and say, 'What are you guys doing?' If it was a bunch of White students or a bunch of Asian students, what does it matter because the university is mostly White and Asian. But because we were Black students, out there together, I guess we're a threat of some type. Things like that, it's always something like that that you have to deal with. (Jahzara, native Black female, third-year student)

She gave a poignant example of being made to feel that Black students do not belong on campus. She also asserted that the university does not acknowledge that poor students may lack the social support of their family. In her experience, many Black students don't have support from home because their families may have other problems or may be struggling financially.

> If you don't have anybody that's retaining you here [college], and being your support system here, it's going to be very hard to finish or get through. The whole idea of fighting for things that we need, the university needs to understand that people have different experiences. Black people have different experiences than white people. People don't know. People don't know. People are ignorant to what goes on in a situation of poverty and how that type of environment affects people. (Jahzara)

Jahzara's parents are divorced and her father is incarcerated. Her mother is a medical administrator. Jahzara's observation is bolstered by the findings in Chapter 2, that Black students come from less economically-advantaged families than do White or Asian students (Figures 2.5 and 2.6).

Black students are more likely to have to deal with administrative offices such as Financial Aid, since the statistics show that Black students are not as well-off as their non-Black counterparts (Figure 2.7). Abike said she was frustrated with the bureaucracy at her school:

> It's not blatant, it's just like, 'Why are there six African American people in line at the Financial Aid Office and no one else?' From last semester, I went to a junior college. I took classes at a JC and I had the transcripts sent here three times. And they 'lost' all three of them, so I don't know how that's possible. And two times they were like 'Attention' to a certain person, so I don't really know how it's possible, but then after I complained to the head of that department, they all three were magically found. So, I don't know, I just don't know, it doesn't make sense to me how stuff like that happens. (Abike, Nigerian American female, third-year student)

She attributed these bureaucratic problems with her race.

In Chapter 4, the supportive function of the Black student community was apparent. There are few Black students on campus so Black students feel they need the support of their ethnic-based student group. Interviewees described the "catch-22" they found when navigating the politics of campus-supported student groups. Institutional funds are dispersed to student groups based, in part, on the size of the group. Black student groups found it difficult to get funding because of their small numbers. Yet Black students have an acute need for these groups because of their small numbers on campus.

Robel, an Eritrean student, gave an example of a Black pre-medical group on campus requesting funds from the university's student government:

> You see certain groups come before you and they're sororities and fraternities and they're putting on these functions and they

[student government] are giving them money, however much they're asking for. We're asking for [money for] a medical conference and they give us less than they're giving these people to throw charity events, which are legitimate causes and I don't have any problem with that. But they don't see the issues we deal with as being of equal merit. They make us feel like we're not as valued by reducing our funding constantly and not making us feel welcome in the [student government]. (Robel, Eritrean male, fourth-year student)

Native and immigrant Black interviewees had similar experiences of feeling questioned, misunderstood, and disenfranchised by the university. These feelings block intellectual integration of Black students on campus.

DISCUSSION

It is clear from the statistical data that there is an overrepresentation of immigrant Blacks in UC schools. The overrepresentation of immigrant Blacks among Black college students is often interpreted as a cultural phenomenon (Hagy and Staniec 2002, Glick and White 2004) in addition to a product of disparities in socioeconomic status (Bennett and Lutz 2009). The data in this study are limited since they are restricted to those who are already UC students. However, findings from the interviews with Black college students demonstrate a narrative of cultural difference between immigrant and native Blacks. It is these differences that young Black college students use to understand the disproportionate numbers of immigrant Blacks in college. Although it is clear from empirical studies that the great differences in socioeconomic status play a larger role, perhaps even explaining the immigrant advantage completely (Bennett and Lutz 2009), it is noteworthy that Black students themselves interpret the disparity in cultural terms.

The narrative of difference can be framed using concepts from the literature on immigrant advantage in education. I found that immigrant Black students exhibit a positive dual frame of reference, wherein the educational system in the U.S. is viewed as an opportunity to be held tightly. The immigrant Blacks also speak of positive social capital from their parents and co-ethnic communities. Native Black students also echoed the theories of cultural difference, describing a negative dual frame of reference, wherein their education and opportunities were considered paltry. However, native Black respondents did not fit into current theories of cultural difference in terms of social capital. Many native Black students have strong parental social capital, which encourages them to pursue post-secondary education. In addition, native Blacks create pro-school social capital in their peer networks.

Less well-studied than college matriculation are the college experiences and graduation rates of immigrant and native Blacks. Massey and colleagues (2007) found no difference in college grade point average between immigrant and native Blacks. In this study, I found no difference in the graduation rates of immigrant versus native Blacks. An explanation for these similarities is that the experience of native Black college students and immigrant Black college students are similar. This supports the thesis of a common Black student experience that goes beyond family immigration history.

The institution of the university treats Black students the same, regardless of family immigration history. The reaction to this treatment is a disassociation with the university, a lack of intellectual integration. Without intellectual integration, Black students are less likely to graduate. Findings from the quantitative data support this hypothesis. Intellectual integration is a significant predictor of Black student graduation and accounts for a portion of the Black-White gap in graduation rates. It is important to note that academic achievement affects intellectual integration, resulting in a bi-directional causal model. Analysis of the qualitative data similarly bolsters the importance of intellectual integration. Black students, immigrant and native, described the ways they felt unsupported and misunderstood by agents of the university.

Contributing to the idea of a unique Black student experience, I found that Black students are less likely to be intellectually integrated than non-Black students (Figure 3.2). Even accounting for background, high school, and campus factors, Black students are less likely than White students to feel a sense of belonging on campus. These findings support the thesis that the Black student experience is different from and worse than that of non-Black students.

CHAPTER 7

Supporting Black College Students

LOOKING FOR DIFFERENCES

I began this project explicitly juxtaposing immigrant Blacks with native Blacks. Segmented assimilation theory suggests that children of immigrants, even those in low-income neighborhoods, benefit from a protective family and co-ethnic community. These social structures propel the second-generation immigrants to achieve academically. The theory of immigrant versus involuntary minorities predicts that those with immigrant backgrounds will be optimistic and motivated to succeed, while native minorities will develop an oppositional culture. These theories are not exactly right for the population in this study since the students in this study have reached the highest echelon of the three-tiered higher education system in California, the University of California. These young people could hardly have an oppositional stance toward schooling.

It is not that I expected native Black college students to perform poorly. UC students have successfully navigated high school, completed the necessary math, English, science, and foreign language requirements, and been recommended by their high school teachers. Native Black UC students have an average high school grade point average of 3.6 out of 4.0. However, Black college students all over the country, whether at selective or less selective colleges, have a lower graduation rate than White and Asian students (Melguizo 2008). Immigrant Black students may have some advantage over native Black students. Their optimism in the face of discrimination, the encouragement (or pressure, as some might describe it) from their families and communities, and their belief that America is a meritocracy might give them an edge over native Black students.

Immigrant Black college students might have an *immigrant advantage* that would help them to excel in college and graduate. And so, I was looking for the possibility of an immigrant advantage rather than a native disadvantage. Although they are two sides of the same coin, there is a difference. Framing the question to look for advantage rather than deficit does not problematize native Blacks but inspects the social structures, economic conditions, and context of reception of immigrant Blacks.

I set out to compare immigrant Black students with native Black students. Interview respondents stressed the differences between immigrant Blacks and native Blacks, in culture, outlook, family values, ethnic community, and especially regarding views on education. Despite narratives of cultural difference, I found that there is a *Black college experience*.

FINDING SIMILARITIES

The experiences and outcomes of immigrant Blacks and native Blacks converge in college. In Chapter 5, the results show that immigrant and native Black college students perceive discrimination on campus in similar ways and at similar rates. As described in Chapter 3, both groups share an overarching feeling of not belonging on campus. In Chapter 4, I present the finding that immigrant and native Black students have similar rates of social integration on campus and similar frequency of interethnic interactions. Interview respondents described a cohesive Black student network that bridged differences in family immigration history. In these ways, a *Black college experience* emerged from the statistical and qualitative data.

Immigrant and native Black students also had similar outcomes. The expected immigrant advantage in post-secondary education was not borne out. There was no difference in college grade point average or graduation rates of immigrant versus native Blacks. I then explored how the Black college experience is different from and less educationally advantageous than the experience of non-Black students.

UNIQUE BLACK COLLEGE EXPERIENCE

The Black college experience described in the preceding section is unique to Black students. That is, on many measures of college experience, Black students stand out from all other ethnic groups. Their experiences are different from White and Asian students', but they are also different than the experiences of Chicano/Latino students. This finding speaks to the question of how the color line is drawn on college campuses, as I discuss in Chapter 3.

With increasing numbers of Latino and Asian people in the U.S., one of the most pressing current social questions is: What are the crucial divides among ethnic groups? These divides are social, and can be measured in rates of intermarriage or residential segregation. They are also economic, as in disparities in wages. Most relevant to this research are the racial and ethnic gaps in educational attainment.

In America's history, there have been sharp differences between Whites and Blacks. Because California is home to huge numbers of immigrant families relative to their numbers in the nation at large, the way that ethnic groups relate in California may presage national race relations. Exploring ethnic relations within the UC system tests the new color line. The similarities in the college experiences and networks of immigrant and native Black students, and the difference between Black student experiences versus those of non-Black students suggest that the color line on UC campuses is between Black and non-Black. Black students are less likely to feel respected, less likely to feel they belong, and less likely to graduate than students of other ethnicities. Despite the gross underrepresentation of Latinos in the UC system, their college experiences are closer to those of White students than to those of Black students.

According to the prevailing model of college student persistence, a student's integration into the college is critical to graduation (Tinto 1993). The two aspects of integration that Tinto (1993) identifies are social and intellectual. I found that Black UC students differ from students of other ethnicities on these two important types of integration.

The unique Black college experience is different from and less desirable than the experience of non-Black students. Chapters 5 and 6 present the case that Black students perceive an omnipresent threat of discrimination and a generalized feeling that they did not belong on campus. The quantitative data in these chapters generalize these perceptions beyond the interview campus. Black students, more than students of other ethnicities, do not feel respected on campus. They are more likely than students of other ethnicities to perceive discrimination from their classmates, professors, and university administrators. The qualitative data shows that discrimination is prevalent and may have a negative effect on academic performance. Black students are also less likely than students of other ethnicities to be intellectually integrated on campus. The qualitative data suggests that Black students felt unsupported and misunderstood by the agents and policies of the university.

A puzzle arises from the social capital results in Chapter 4. Black students have high levels of bonding and bridging social capital, which means they belong to dense and varied networks on campus. And yet, their graduation rates are very low. An aspect of the unique Black college experience is high levels of social capital. Black students were more likely than non-Black students to be members of and participate weekly in student groups. From the qualitative data, it is clear that the Black student network was an important social and academic resource. The Black student community is such a critical aspect of Black students' college experience that their path of social integration is shaped by whether they belong to it, are branching out of it, or are consciously apart from it. When interviewees talk about their place in the social structure of the university, they define it in terms of the Black student community, even if they do not belong to it. Black students were also more likely to have in-depth conversations with students of other ethnicities. Such social integration has traditionally been seen as beneficial to persistence in college (Tinto 1993). Yet Black students have the lowest graduation rate of any ethnic group.

The unique Black college experience results in tangible deficits in academic attainment. Black students have high levels of social integration, which is widely-held to be an important factor contributing to college persistence. Yet social capital variables are not significant in models of Black student persistence. On the other hand, Black students are the least intellectually integrated ethnic group on college campuses. Intellectual integration variables *are* significant in models of Black student persistence.

It is important to work toward a theoretical model of college attrition that recognizes the unique experience of Black students. Black students seem to be doing the right thing by participating in on-campus groups, by socially integrating into the university. According to both the statistical and qualitative data, this effort on the part of Black students is often met with indifference on the part of the institution. It is Black students' lack of intellectual integration that at least partially accounts for the low graduation rate of Black students compared with students of other ethnicities.

I began this project with the idea that differences in educational attainment might be caused by culture. And that is what I found. But it is not immigrant culture or Black culture causing the disparities. It is the *culture* of the institution, the *culture* of the college classroom, the *culture* of the campus. It is telling that non-Black students largely believe that students are respected on their college campus regardless of race or ethnicity. Black students attempt to survive and excel in an environment of unacknowledged racism to which other students are oblivious. These factors contribute to a unique and uniquely disadvantageous Black college experience that leads to low rates of persistence. Whether measured by selectivity or diversity, the institution has consistently been a significant factor in determining the social experience and educational outcomes of all students.

IMPROVING BLACK GRADUATION RATES

Institutions of higher education in the United States face a daunting challenge: to educate the next generation of leaders in this fast-changing, global environment. Countries such as China and India are creating an educated and economically-competitive workforce. Jobs that were formerly filled by American workers are now being moved overseas, thanks to improvements in global communication. Educators in the United States are right to be concerned about these developments, especially given the low college graduation rates of the increasing Black and Latino populations. In this section, I present policy recommendations aimed at increasing the persistence of Black students in college.

The unique Black college experience affects graduation rates. Controlling for family socioeconomic status, gender, immigrant generation, high school performance, and college selectivity, Black students are less likely to graduate than White students. Black students have the lowest graduation rate of all ethnic groups. This gap is partially explained by intellectual integration as well as campus selectivity. Thus, the institution plays a measurable role in Black student attrition. This also means that the institution can play a measurable role in Black student persistence.

An institutional factor that contributes to the unique Black college experience is ethnic diversity. The results of this study suggest that increasing the share of Black students will have a salutary effect on the probability that Black students will feel respected and will have a sense of belonging on campus, as discussed in Chapter 3. In Chapter 4, I argued that Black students turn to each other for empathetic understanding of the unique and disadvantaged situation in which Blacks on campus find themselves. Universities can take positive steps to increase the numbers of admitted Black students who matriculate to campus. For example, during the 2009-2010 academic year, UC San Diego announced initiatives to boost the enrollment of admitted minority students. These included a student, faculty, staff, and alumni phone campaign to reach out to admitted minority students, as well as an overnight program for prospective Black students. Such programs were already in place at other campuses. With greater numbers of Blacks on campus, there is an increase in the social support necessary for Blacks to succeed. Improving Black students' experiences will enhance their commitment to the university and chances of eventual graduation.

When there is financial support for student groups, the funds should be dispersed based on merit or need, rather than numbers. Black students are more likely than students of other ethnicities to belong to and lead student groups, and spend time on these groups every week. Black students also feel an obligation to participate in campus groups, to increase their visibility and create a sense of camaraderie. Institutional policies can undermine minority groups when funding is based on numbers. The Black student network provides social and academic support. Penalizing a Black group because they don't have enough members is nonsensical. Black students need these groups *because* they are underrepresented. They feel that the university does not support them and does not understand their unique plight. This also marginalizes Black groups on campus. Student groups that primarily serve underrepresented minorities *can* be drawn into the mainstream life of the campus. Since the passage of Proposition 209, banning preferences based on race, sex, color, ethnicity, or national origin, some UC campuses modified programs to serve students who have overcome disadvantaged social or economic backgrounds. For example, at UC Davis, preference is given to student groups that advance the institutional goal of campus diversity, broadly understood. Institutional funding is an expedient and compelling show of support for groups that are composed of underrepresented minorities.

University administrators, student services personnel, and instructors can find ways to encourage peer-to-peer interethnic interactions. These interactions would allow students of different ethnicities to be on equal footing as they meet, exchange ideas, live together, and study together. A practical suggestion that arose from the interview data was to address forming study groups in class. Graduate student instructors and professors should be aware of the anxiety that Black students may have around forming groups. When dividing classes into groups, instructors could assign students rather than asking them to choose group members. This allows all students to come together as equals in a working group.

Another suggestion would be to improve the efficiency of the Financial Aid Office. Over 70% of Black UC students use the Financial Aid Office, compared to less than half of White or Asian students. The frustrations that the interview respondents in this study voiced about administrative offices, is borne disproportionately by Black and Chicano/Latino students. This is especially important in light of the $500 million reduction in state support to the UC system, approved by the California legislature in March 2011 (Buchanan and Lagos 2011).

There is a Black college experience; it transcends immigrant generation; it has an impact on academic attainment; and it can be manipulated by institutional policies. Black students have a qualitatively different and less advantageous college experiences than other minority students. The legacy of slavery in the U.S. is such that race remains a crucial social fact in daily interactions. Although there is growing heterogeneity within Blacks in America, race remains an impermeable boundary that immigrant Blacks find they cannot cross.

As long as U.S. society continues to treat all Blacks as equal to each other and as unequal to the other members of society, then differentiation within the Black community will be disadvantageous. In this study, immigrant Blacks said they were seen as and treated the same as native Blacks. They cope by embracing a common Black identity and strengthening the common Black community. They downplay intra-group differences. As detailed in Chapters 5 and 6, Black students are attempting to thrive in a racially hostile environment. They are beset with discrimination from peers, instructors, and administrators. The hope for change lies with evidence-based programs that will support Black students as they integrate into the mainstream social and intellectual life of the campus.

Table of Interview Respondents

Pseudonym	Gender	Ethnicity	Father's educational attainment	Mother's educational attainment
Maurice	Male	African American	Bachelor's degree	Bachelor's degree
Robert	Male	Jewish	High school diploma	Associate's degree
James	Male	Black	High school diploma	Associate's degree
Bradley	Male	African American	High school diploma	High school diploma
Mary	Female	Black or African American	Associate's degree	High school diploma
Brandi	Female	African descent	Bachelor's degree	Bachelor's degree
Imani	Female	African American	10th grade	Graduate degree
Shanice	Female	African American	Associate's degree	High school diploma
Aaliyah	Female	Black or African American	Bachelor's degree	Bachelor's degree
Jada	Female	Black	High school diploma	High school diploma
Kiara	Female	Black	High school diploma	High school diploma

Pseudonym	Gender	Ethnicity	Father's educational attainment	Mother's educational attainment
Latoya	Female	Black	Bachelor's degree	Graduate degree
Jasmin	Female	Black	High school diploma	Bachelor's degree
Alexis	Female	African American	Bachelor's degree	High school diploma
Raven	Female	African American	High school diploma	Bachelor's degree
Sherice	Female	Black	High school diploma	Associate's degree
Ayana	Female	Black	High school diploma	High school diploma
Jahzara	Female	Black	Associate's degree	Associate's degree
Kim	Female	African American	Graduate degree	Bachelor's degree
Bekele	Male	Ethiopian	High school diploma	High school diploma
Bin	Male	Ethiopian and Filipino	Bachelor's degree	Associate's degree
Tekle	Male	Ethiopian	High school diploma	High school diploma
Makeda	Female	Ethiopian	Graduate degree	Bachelor's degree
Amara	Female	Ethiopian	Bachelor's degree	9th grade
Dele	Male	Nigerian American	Bachelor's degree	Associate's degree
Oladapo	Male	Nigerian	Bachelor's degree	Bachelor's degree
Abike	Female	Nigerian American	Bachelor's degree	Bachelor's degree
Ozioma	Female	Nigerian American	Bachelor's degree	Bachelor's degree

Pseudonym	Gender	Ethnicity	Father's educational attainment	Mother's educational attainment
Ezinne	Female	Nigerian American	Graduate degree	Bachelor's degree
Adenike	Female	Nigerian American	Graduate degree	Graduate degree
Titilayo	Female	Nigerian American	Bachelor's degree	High school diploma
Nicole	Female	Nigerian and African American	Graduate degree	Bachelor's degree
Nnenna	Female	Nigerian	Graduate degree	Graduate degree
Eniola	Female	Nigerian American	Graduate degree	Graduate degree
Itunu	Female	Nigerian	Graduate degree	Bachelor's degree
Chika	Female	Nigerian	Graduate degree	Graduate degree
Samir	Male	Sudanese	Graduate degree	Graduate degree
Robel	Male	Eritrean	High school diploma	High school diploma
Erica	Female	Eritrean	Associate's degree	9th grade

Native Blacks – Gray shaded (n = 19)
Immigrant Blacks – No shading (n = 20)

Questionnaire

Date	
Informant #	

- Consent form
- Stipend
- Multiple-choice, short answer
- Detailed questions – record
- Questions?

1. What is your gender?   Male 0
                           Female 1

2. What is your race?
   American Indian and Alaska Native 1
   Asian 2
   Black or African American 3
   Native Hawaiian and Other Pacific Islander 4
   White 5
   Other 6

3. How would you describe your ethnicity?   _____

4. In what month and year were you born?

Month MM	Year YYYY

5. Did you ever get a GED or a high school diploma?

	No 0	
	GED 1	
Date Earned	Month	Year
	HS Diploma 2	

Name of high school graduated from _____

City, State _____

Graduation	Month	Year

6. What was your high school GPA?

weighted ☐

unweighted ☐

7. Do you have any college degrees?

No 0

Associate's Degree 1

Bachelor's Degree 2

Other 3

Specify:

8. What school do you currently attend? _____

Full-time 1

Part-time 2

9. What semester and year did you start at this school?

Semester	Year

10. Were you born in America?

Yes 1 ☐ *Go to question 14*

No 0 ☐ *Go to question 11*

11. Where were you born?

                    Country   _____

12. How old were you when you immigrated? (years)   _____

13. What is your citizenship status?

                            Citizen 1   ☐
                            Green card 2   ☐
                            Visa 3   ☐
                            Other 4   ☐

14. Where was your mother born?   Country   _____

15. Where was your father born?   Country   _____

16. Where was your mother's mother born?   Country   _____

17. Where was your mother's father born?   Country   _____

18. Where was your father's mother born?   Country   _____

19. Where was your father's father born?   Country   _____

20. What is the highest grade in elementary school or high school that your father completed and got credit for?

No formal schooling	0	
1st grade	1	
2nd grade	2	
3rd grade	3	
4th grade	4	
5th grade	5	
6th grade	6	
7th grade	7	
8th grade	8	
9th grade	9	
10th grade	10	
11th grade	11	
12th grade	12	

22. Did your father ever get a GED or high school diploma?

No 0	
Yes 1	

23. Does your father have any college degrees?

No	0
Yes	1

Associate/Junior college	1	
Bachelor's	2	
Graduate	3	

24. Was his highest degree attained in

U.S.	1
Abroad	2

Specify country _____

25. What is the highest grade in elementary school or high school that your mother completed and got credit for?

No formal schooling	0	
1st grade	1	
2nd grade	2	
3rd grade	3	
4th grade	4	
5th grade	5	
6th grade	6	
7th grade	7	
8th grade	8	
9th grade	9	
10th grade	10	
11th grade	11	
12th grade	12	

26. Did your mother ever get a GED or high school diploma?

No 0	
Yes 1	

27. Does your mother have any college degrees?

No	0	
Yes	1	

Associate/Junior college	1	
Bachelor's	2	
Graduate	3	

28. Was her highest degree attained in

U.S.	1	
Abroad	2	

Specify country _____

29. What is your parents' marital
    status?
Never married	1	
Married	2	
Separated	3	
Divorced	4	

    Whom do you primarily live with? _____

30. What is your best estimate of the household
    income, where you live?

Less than $9,999	1	
$10,000 - $39,999	2	
$40,000 - $79,999	3	
$80,000 - $119,999	4	
$120,000 - $149,999	5	
$150,000 - $179,999	6	
Over $180,000	7	

If parent(s) immigrated, answer question 31.
If both parents are native born, go to question 32.

31. What did your parents do in [home country]?
Father	
Mother	

32. What do your parents do for a living now?
Father	
Mother	

33. Do your parents rent or own
    their home?

Rent	1	
Own	2	

34. To pay for your tuition, do you   Yes 1   No 0
have

Scholarship(s)		
Loan(s)		
Parent(s) paying		
Savings		
Job(s)		

35. What about living expenses   Yes 1   No 0

Scholarship(s)		
Loan(s)		
Parent(s) paying		
Savings		
Job(s)		

36. Would you say that the financial package you received is

Excellent	1	
Fair	2	
Poor	3	

37. Is a language other than English spoken in your home?

No 0

Yes 1

Language   _____

38. Do you have brothers, sisters, half-brothers/ sisters, or step-brothers/sisters?

Yes 1 ☐ *Go to question 39*

No 0 ☐ *Go to question 40*

39. How old are each of them?
    [If old siblings are old enough] How far did they go in school?

Brother or sister	Age	Highest Degree Earned	Name of college

40. How far would you like to go in school?

Some college	1	
Technical/vocational school	2	
Associate's degree	3	
Bachelor's degree	4	
Graduate degree	5	

41. How far do you expect you'll go in school?

Some college	1	
Technical/vocational school	2	
Associate's degree	3	
Bachelor's degree	4	
Graduate degree	5	

42. Did you take the SAT I and what were your scores?
    Didn't take the SAT_____

	First time	Second time	Third time
Score			

43. Compared to the average [*informant's college*] student, how would you rate your academic ability?

Well above average	
Somewhat above average	
Average	
Somewhat below average	
Well below average	

44. What clubs or groups do you belong to on campus?

In-Depth Questions

College experience – General

1. What's been the hardest thing about college?
2. What's your favorite thing about college?
3. Have you ever thought about transferring to another school?
4. Have you ever thought about not finishing college?
5. Do you ever worry about having enough money to finish college?

Identity

6. I'd like you to think about your three closest friends. What is their racial or ethnic background?
7. You said that your racial/ethnic identity is [*informant's racial identity*]. Does that identity change based on the situation you're in?
8. Tell me about the [*African American/ Nigerian/ Ethiopian*] community when you were growing up.

Discrimination

9. Since you've started school here, have you ever felt like someone was showing prejudice toward you or discriminating against you?
10. Do you ever feel uncomfortable on campus because you're [*informant's ethnicity*]?

Follow up: Can you give me an example?

Perceptions of professors and graduate student instructors

11. Do you talk to any of your professors outside of class? [Probe for relationship with faculty]

12. How do you believe your professors perceive your ability compared with other students?

Graduate Student Instructors
13. Do you talk to any of your GSIs outside of class?
14. How do you believe your GSIs perceive your ability compared with other students?

Perceptions of classmates
15. How do you think your classmates perceive your ability compared with the other students?

Follow up: Do their perceptions affect the way you act?

Gender

Sometimes parents push boys harder in school. In other families, girls are expected to do better academically.
16. What is it like in your family? [Probe for example]
17. What are your brothers doing now?
18. Think about the African American boys you knew growing up (in your neighborhood, elementary school). What are they doing now?
19. Is this much different from what the African American girls you knew are doing?

African Americans and Black Immigrants
20. Not just on campus, but in general, have you noticed differences between Black Americans and *[informant's ethnicity; if African American, "black immigrants like Nigerians"]*?

Follow up: Have you noticed differences in terms of attitudes towards education?

21. Do you think that other people, like White Americans see the difference between African Americans and Black immigrants?

Follow-Up Questionnaire

Confidential Form
Please do not type your name on this form. The information you provide on this form, as well as your interview data, is kept anonymous. Your unique informant # is the code that I use to identify you.

Informant #

Questions

1. What is your enrollment status at UC campus for Spring 2009? Please check one.

   ☐ Full-time student
   ☐ Part-time student

   Graduated
   Term of graduation (fall or spring)
       Year of graduation

   Not enrolled

2. If "part-time student" or "not enrolled," what are you doing?

3. What was (is) your GPA at UC campus?

4. How would you describe your religion?

Instructions
Send the completed form to aathomas@fas.harvard.edu

Conclusion
Thanks so much for your time today and also doing the interview last year. If you have any questions, feel free to contact me by e-mail or phone.

References

Ainsworth-Darnell, James W. and Douglas B. Downey. 1998. "Assessing the Oppositional Culture Explanation for Racial/Ethnic Differences in School Performance." *American Sociological Review* 63:536-553.

Alba, Richard and Victor Nee. 2003. *Remaking the American Mainstream: Assimilation and contemporary immigration.* Cambridge, MA: Harvard University Press.

Allen, Walter R. 1985. "Black Student, White Campus: Structural, Interpersonal, and Psychological Correlates of Success." *Journal of Negro Education* 54:134-147.

Allen, Walter R. 1992. "The Color of Success: African American college student outcomes at pre-dominantly White and historically Black colleges and universities." *Harvard Educational Review* 62:26-44.

Antonio, Anthony Lising, Mitchell J. Chang, Kenji Hakuta, David A. Kenny, Shana Levin, and Jeffrey F. Milem. 2004. "Effects of Racial Diversity on Complex Thinking in College Students." *Psychological Science* 15:507-510.

Bailey, Martha J. and Susan M. Dynarski. 2011. "Gains and Gaps: Changing Inequality in U.S. College Entry and Completion." NBER Working Paper No. 17633. National Bureau of Economic Research. Accessed online February 14, 2013: http://www.nber.org/papers/w17633

Baker, Therese L. and William Velez. 1996. "Access to and Opportunity in Postsecondary Education in the United States: A Review." *Sociology of Education* 69:82-101.

Bankston, Carl L. and Min Zhou. 1995. "Effects of Minority-Language Literacy on the Academic Achievement of Vietnamese Youths in New Orleans." *Sociology of Education* 68:1-17.

Bauman, Kurt J. and Nikki L. Graf. 2003. "Educational Attainment: 2000." U.S. Census Bureau, Washington, DC.

Bean, John P. 1985. "Interaction Effects Based on Class Level in an Explanatory Model of College Student Dropout Syndrome." *American Educational Research Journal* 22:35-64.

Beattie, Irenee R. 2002. "Are All "Adolescent Econometricians" Created Equal? Racial, Class, and Gender Differences in College Enrollment." *Sociology of Education* 75:19-43.

Bennett, Pamela R. and Amy Lutz. 2009. "How African American is the Net Black Advantage? Differences in College Attendance Among Immigrant Blacks, Native Blacks, and Whites." *Sociology of Education* 82:70-99.

Bowen, William G. and Derek Curtis Bok. 2000. *The Shape of the River : Long-Term Consequences of Considering Race in College and University Admissions*. Princeton, N.J.: Princeton University Press.

Brubaker, Rogers. 2009. "Ethnicity, Race, and Nationalism." *Annual Review of Sociology* 35:21-42.

Buchanan, Wyatt and Marisa Lagos. 2011. "California Legislature passes deep-cuts budget." Pp. A6 in *San Francisco Chronicle*. San Francisco.

Bureau of Labor Statistics. 2005. "Civilian Labor Force Participation Rate by Demographic Characteristic, 1965-2005." vol. 2007: Department of Labor.

Cabrera, A., A. Nora, P. Terenzini, E. Pascarella, L. Hagedorn, and L. Serra. 1999. "Campus racial climate and the adjustment of students to college: A comparison between White students andAfrican-American students." Pp. 134-160 in *Journal of Higher Education*, vol. 70.

Carter, Prudence L. 2005. *Keepin' It Real: School success beyond black and white*. New York: Oxford University Press.

Charmaz, Kathy. 2000. "Grounded Theory: Objectivist and Constructivist Methods." Pp. 509-536 in *Handbook for Qualitative Research*, edited by N. K. Denzin and Y. S. Lincoln. Thousand Oaks, CA: Sage Publications.

Chickering, Arthur W. and Linda Reisser. 1993. *Education and identity*. San Francisco: Jossey-Bass.

Coleman, James S. 1990. "Social Capital." Pp. 300-324 in *Foundations of Social Theory*. Cambridge, MA: Belknap Press.

Coleman, James S. 1988. "Social Capital in the Creation of Human Capital." *The American Journal of Sociology* 94:S95-S120.

Crim, E. J. 1998. "Aversive Racism on Campus: Explaining Mechanisms of Isolation for Students and Staff of Color on Campus." in *The Annual Meeting of the Association for the Study of Higher Education*. Florida.

Davis, Mitzi, Yvonne Dias-Bowie, Katherine Greenberg, Gary Klukken, Howard R. Pollio, Sandra P. Thomas, and Charles L. Thompson. 2004. ""A Fly in the Buttermilk": Descriptions of University Life by Successful Black Undergraduate Students at a Predominately White Southeastern University." *The Journal of Higher Education* 75:420-445.

Deaux, Kay, Nida Bikmen, Alwyn Gilkes, Ana Ventuneac, Yvanne Joseph, Yasser A. Payne, and Claude M. Steele. 2007. "Becoming American: Stereotype Threat Effects in Afro-Caribbean Immigrant Groups." *Social Psychology Quarterly* 70:384-404.

Deaux, Kay. 2006. *To Be an Immigrant*. New York: Russell Sage Foundation.

Deil-Amen, Regina and Ruth Lopez Turley. 2007. "A Review of the Transition to College Literature in Sociology." *Teachers College Record* 109:2324-2366.

Djamba, Yanyi K. 1999. "African Immigrants in the United States: A Socio-Demographic Profile in Comparison to Native Blacks." *Journal of Asian and African Studies* 34:210-215.

Dodoo, F. Nii-Amoo. 1997. "Assimilation Differences among Africans in America." *Social Forces* 76:527-46.

Dovidio, John F., Samuel L. Gaertner, Yolanda Flores Niemann, and Kevin Snider. 2001. "Racial, Ethnic, and Cultural Differences in Responding to Distinctiveness and Discrimination on Campus: Stigma and Common Group Identity." *Journal of Social Issues* 57:167-188.

Espenshade, Thomas and Alexandria Walton Radford. 2009. *No Longer Separate, Not Yet Equal: Race and class in elite colleges admission and campus life*. Princeton and Oxford: Princeton University Press.

Feagin, Joe R. 1992. "The Continuing Significance of Racism: Discrimination Against Black Students in White Colleges." *Journal of Black Studies* 22:546-578.

Feliciano, Cynthia. 2006. "Beyond the Family: The influence of premigration group status on the educational expectations of immigrants' children." *Sociology of Education* 79:281-303.

Fine, Michelle and Pearl Rosenberg. 1983. "Dropping Out of High School: The ideology of school and work." *Journal of Education* 165:257-272.

Fletcher, Sandra E. 2012. "Personal and Institutional Factors: Relationship to self-efficacy of persistence to the senior year in college among self-identified Black undergraduate students in a Hispanic Serving Institution." *FIU Electronic Theses and Dissertations.* Paper 703. Accessed online February 14, 2013: http://digitalcommons.fiu.edu/etd/703

Fordham, Signithia and John Ogbu. 1986. "Black Students' School Success: Coping with the "burden of 'acting White'"." *The Urban Review* 18:176-206.

Galligani, Dennis J. 2003. "Information Digest 2003." University of California Office of the President, Oakland, CA.

Gansemer-Topf, Ann M. and John H. Schuh. 2006. "Institutional Selectivity and Institutional Expenditures: Examining Organizational Factors that Contribute to Retention and Graduation." *Research in Higher Education* 47:613-642.

Gerdes, Hillary and Brent Mallinckrodt. 1994. "Emotional, Social, and Academic Adjustment of College Students: A longitudinal study of retention." *Journal of Counseling & Development* 72:281-287.

Geshekter, Charles L. 2008. "The Effects of Proposition 209 on California: Higher education, public employment, and contracting." in *Race and Gender Preferences at the Crossroads.* University of Southern California: California Association of Scholars and American Civil Rights Institute.

Gibson, Margaret. 1988. *Accommodation Without Assimilation*. Ithaca, NY: Cornell University Press.

Glaser, Barney G. and Anselm L. Strauss. 1967. *The Discovery of Grounded Theory: Strategies for qualitative research.* New York: Aldine de Gruyter.

Glick, Jennifer E. and Michael J. White. 2004. "Post-Secondary School Participation of Immigrant and Native Youth: The Role of Familial Resources and Educational Expectations." *Social Science Research* 33:272.

Gordon, Milton. 1964. *Assimilation in American Life.* New York: Oxford University Press.

Granovetter, Mark S. 1973. "The Strength of Weak Ties." *American Journal of Sociology* 78:1360-1380.

Grant, G. K. and J. R. Breese. 1997. "Marginality theory and the African American student." *Sociology of Education* 70:192-205.

Hagy, Alison P. and J. Farley Ordovensky Staniec. 2002. "Immigrant Status, Race, and Institutional Choice in Higher Education." *Economics of Education Review* 21:381-392.

Harper, Shaun R. and Sylvia Hurtado. 2007. "Nine themes in campus racial climates and implications for institutional transformation." *New Directions for Student Services*:7-24.

Harper, Shaun R. and Stephen John. Quaye. 2007. "Student Organizations as Venues for Black Identity Expression and Development among African American Male Student Leaders." *Journal of College Student Development* 48:127-144.

Hauser, Robert M. and Douglas K. Anderson. 1991. "Post-High School Plans and Aspirations of Black and White High School Seniors: 1976-86." *Sociology of Education* 64:263-277.

Hershberger, Scott L. and Anthony R. D'augeiti. 1992. "The Relationship of Academic Performance and Social Support to Graduation Among African-American and White University Students: A Path-Analytic Model." *Journal of Community Psychology* 20:188-199.

Hinrichs, Peter. 2012. "The Effects of Affirmative Action Bans on College Enrollment, Educational Attainment, and the Demographic Composition of Universities." *The Review of Economics and Statistics* 94:712-722.

Hughes, Everett Cherrington. 1945. "Dilemmas and Contradictions of Status." *The American Journal of Sociology* 50:353-359.

Jones, Terry. 1998. "Life after proposition 209." *Academe* 84:22.

Kane, Thomas J. 1994. "College entry by Blacks since 1970 : the role of college costs, family background and the returns to education." Pp. 33 p. in *Faculty research working paper series; R94-07.* Cambridge, MA: Research Programs John F. Kennedy School of Government Harvard University.

Kao, Grace and Jennifer S. Thompson. 2003. "Racial and Ethnic Stratification in Educational Achievement and Attainment." *Annual Review of Sociology* 29:417-443.

Kao, Grace and Marta Tienda. 1998. "Educational Aspirations of Minority Youth." *American Journal of Education* 106:349-384.

Karabel, Jerome. 1999. "The Rise and Fall of Affirmative Action at the University of California." *The Journal of Blacks in Higher Education* 25:109-112.

Kasinitz, Philip. 1992. "From a Presence to a Community: New York's West Indian Neighborhoods." Pp. 38-89 in *Caribbean New York: Black Immigrants and the Politics of Race.* Ithaca: Cornell University Press.

Kasinitz, Philip, John H. Mollenkopf, Mary C. Waters, and Jennifer Holdaway. 2008. *Inheriting the City: The Children of Immigrants Come of Age.* New York: Russell Sage Foundation.

Kleinfeld, Judith. 1999. "Student performance: males versus females." *Public Interest*:3.

Lee, Jennifer and Frank D. Bean. 2007. "Reinventing the Color Line Immigration and America's New Racial/Ethnic Divide." *Social Forces* 86:561-586.

Lee, Stacey J. 1996. *Unraveling the "Model Minority" Stereotype: Listening to Asian American youth.* New York: Teachers College Press.

Leonhardt, David. 2012, October 14. "Rethinking Affirmative Action." *New York Times*, p. SR4.

Levin, Shana, Colette Van Laar, and Winona Foote. 2006. "Ethnic Segregation and Perceived Discrimination in College: Mutual Influences and Effects on Social and Academic Life." *Journal of Applied Social Psychology* 36:1471-1501.

Logan, John R. and Glenn Deane. 2003. "Black Diversity in Metropolitan America." Lewis Mumford Center.

Lovett, Ian. 2011. "U.C.L.A. Student's Video Rant Against Asians Fuels Firestorm." Pp. A21 in *New York Times.* New York City.

Maitre, Michelle. 2005. "UC Berkeley Raises Red Flags about Prop. 209." in *Oakland Tribune*. Oakland, CA.

Mallinckrodt, Brent. 1988. "Student retention, social support, and dropout intention: Comparison of Black and White students." *Journal of College Student Development* 29:60-64.

Massey, Douglas S., Margarita Mooney, Kimberly C. Torres, and Camille Z. Charles. 2007. "Black Immigrants and Black Natives Attending Selective Colleges and Universities in the United States." *American Journal of Education* 113:243-271.

Massey, Douglas S. 2007. *Categorically Unequal: The American Stratification System*. New York: Russell Sage.

McDaniel, Anne, Thomas A. DiPrete, Claudia Buchmann, and Uri Shwed. 2011. "The Black Gender Gap in Educational Attainment: Historical Trends and Racial Comparisons." *Demography* 48:889-914.

Melguizo, Tatiana. 2008. "Quality Matters: Assessing the Impact of Attending More Selective Institutions on College Completion Rates of Minorities." *Research in Higher Education* 49:214-236.

Mittelberg, David and Mary C. Waters. 1992. "The process of ethnogenesis among Haitian and Israeli immigrants in the United States." *Ethnic & Racial Studies* 15:412.

Murguia, E., R.V. Padilla, and D.M. Pavel. 1991. "Ethnicity and the concept of social integration in Tinto's model of institutional departure." *Journal of College Student Development* 32:433-439.

Murtaugh, Paul A., Leslie D. Burns, and Jill Schuster. 1999. "Predicting the Retention of University Students." *Research in Higher Education* 40:355-371.

Museus, Samuel D. and Dina C. Maramba. 2011. "The Impact of Culture on Filipino American Students' Sense of Belonging." *The Review of Higher Education* 34:231-258.

Museus, Samuel D. 2008. "The Role of Ethnic Student Organizations in Fostering African American and Asian American Students' Cultural Adjustment and Membership at Predominantly White Institutions." *Journal of College Student Development* 49:568-586.

Nadler, Joel T. and M. H. Clark. 2011. "Stereotype Threat: A meta-analysis comparing African Americans to Hispanic Americans." *Journal of Applied Social Psychology* 41:872-890.

Nagasawa, Richard and Paul Wong. 1999. "A Theory of Minority Students' Survival in College." *Sociological Inquiry* 69:76-90.

National Center of Education Statistics 2005. "Digest of Education Statistics 2005: Percentage of persons age 25 to 29, by race/ethnicity, years of school completed: Selected years, 1910 through 2005." vol. 2007.

Ocampo, Carmina. 2006. "Prop 209: Ten Long Years." Pp. 8 in *Nation*, vol. 283: Nation Company, L. P.

Ogbu, John U. 2004. "Collective Identity and the Burden of "Acting White" in Black History, Community, and Education." *Urban Review* 36:1-35.

Ogbu, John. 1991. "Immigrant and Involuntary Minorities in Comparative Perspective." in *Minority Status and Schooling: A comparative study of immigrant and involuntary minorities*, edited by J. Ogbu and M. Gibson. New York: Garland Publishing, Inc.

Ogbu, John U. and Herbert D. Simons. 1998. "Voluntary and Involuntary Minorities: A Cultural-Ecological Theory of School Performance with Some Implications for Education." *Anthropology & Education Quarterly* 29:155-188.

Ogbu, John U. 1987. "Variability in Minority School Performance: A Problem in Search of an Explanation." *Anthropology & Education Quarterly* 18:312-334.

Patterson, Orlando. 2009. "Race and Diversity in the Age of Obama." Pp. BR32 in *New York Times*. New York.

Patterson, Orlando. 1997. *The Ordeal of Integration: Progress and resentment in America's "racial" crisis*. New York: Basic Civitas.

Pewewardy, Cornel and Bruce Frey. 2002. "Surveying the Landscape: Perceptions of Multicultural Support Services and Racial Climate at a Predominantly White University." *The Journal of Negro Education* 71:77-95.

Portes, Alejandro. 1998. "Social Capital: Its Origins and Applications in Modern Sociology." *Annual Review of Sociology* 24:1-24.

Portes, Alejandro and Min Zhou. 1993. "The New Second Generation: Segmented assimilation and its variants." *The Annals of the American Academy of Political and Social Science* 530:74-96.

Portes, Alejandro and Rubén Rumbaut. 2001. *Legacies: The story of the immigrant second generation*. Berkeley: University of California Press.

Price, Douglas B., Adrienne E. Hyle, and Kitty V. Jordan. 2009. "Perpetuation of Racial Comfort and Discomfort at a Community College." *Community College Review* 37:3-33.

Putnam, Robert. 2000. *Bowling Alone*. New York: Simon & Schuster.

Rimer, Sara and Karen W. Arenson. 2004. "Top Colleges Take More Blacks, but Which Ones?" Pp. 1 in *New York Times*. New York.

Robinson, Cedric J. 2001. "The Inventions of the Negro." *Social Identities* 7:329-361.

Rong, Xue Lan and Frank Brown. 2001. "The Effects of Immigrant Generation and Ethnicity on Educational Attainment among Young African and Caribbean Blacks in the United States." *Harvard Educational Review* 71:536-565.

Rumbaut, Rubén G. 1996. "The Crucible Within: Ethnic identity, self-esteem, and segmented assimilation among children of immigrants." Pp. 119-170 in *The New Second Generation*, edited by A. Portes. New York: Russell Sage Foundation.

Schmader, Toni, Brenda Major, and Richard W. Gramzow. 2001. "Coping With Ethnic Stereotypes in the Academic Domain: Perceived Injustice and Psychological Disengagement." *Journal of Social Issues* 57:93-111.

Schneider, Barbara and David Stevenson. 1999. *The Ambitious Generation: America's teenagers motivated but directionless*. New Haven and London: Yale University Press.

Sears, David O., Mingying Fu, P. J. Henry, and Kerra Bui. 2003. "The Origins and Persistence of Ethnic Identity among the "New Immigrant" Groups." *Social Psychology Quarterly* 66:419-437.

Sears, David O. and Victoria Savalei. 2006. "The Political Color Line in America: Many "Peoples of Color" or Black Exceptionalism?" *Political Psychology* 27:895-924.

Smedley, Brian D., Hector F. Myers, and Shelly P. Harrell. 1993. "Minority-status stresses and the college adjustment of ethnic minority freshmen." *Journal of Higher Education* 64:434-452.

Smith, Sandra S. and Mignon R. Moore. 2000. "Intraracial Diversity and Relations among African-Americans: Closeness among Black Students at a Predominantly White University." *American Journal of Sociology* 106:1.

State of California, Department of Finance. 2009. "Ethnic Population Estimates with Age and Sex Detail, 2000-2007." Sacramento, CA.

State of California, Department of Finance, *E-3 Race / Ethnic Population Estimates with Age and Sex Detail, 2000– 2007.*Sacramento, CA, May 2009. Accessed October 14, 2009. http://www.dof.ca.gov/research/demographic/data/e-3

Steele, Claude. 1997. "A Threat in the Air: How stereotypes shape intellectual identity and performance." *American Psychologist* 52:613-629.

Steele, Claude M. and Joshua Aronson. 1995. "Stereotype Threat and the Intellectual Test Performance of African Americans." *Journal of Personality & Social Psychology* 69:797-811.

Steele, Claude M. and Joshua A. Aronson. 2004. "Stereotype Threat Does Not Live by Steele and Aronson (1995) Alone." *American Psychologist* 59:47-48.

Tatum, Beverly Daniel. 1997. *"Why Are All the Black Kids Sitting Together in the Cafeteria?" and Other Conversations about Race.* New York: BasicBooks.

Tauriac, Jesse J. and Joan H. Liem. 2012. "Exploring the Divergent Academic Outcomes of U.S.-Origin and Immigrant-Origin Black Undergradutes." *Journal of Diversity in Higher Education* 5:244- 258.

Taylor, Ronald D., Robin Casten, Susanne M. Flickinger, and Debra Roberts. 1994. "Explaining the School Performance of African-American Adolescents." *Journal of Research on Adolescence* 4:21- 44.

The Education Trust. 2007. "College Results Online." http://www.collegeresults.org, Sept 29, 2007.

Tinto, Vincent. 1993. *Leaving College: Rethinking the Causes and Cures of Student Attrition.* Chicago ; London: University of Chicago Press.

Tinto, Vincent. 1975. "Dropout from Higher Education: A theoretical synthesis of recent research." *Review of Educational Research* 45:89-125.

Tuan, Mia. 1998. *Forever Foreigners or Honorary Whites?: The Asian ethnic experience today.* New Brunswick: Rutgers.

UC Endowment Report. 2004. Office of the Treasurer of the Regents, University of California.

U.S. Census Bureau. 2004a. "Income in the Past 12 Months, 2004 American Community Survey." vol. 2007: U.S. Census Bureau.

U.S. Census Bureau. 2004b. "Income in the Past 12 Months, 2004 American Community Survey, California." vol. 2007: U.S. Census.

U.S. Census Bureau. 1998a. "Selected Characteristics for Persons of Nigerian Ancestry: 1990." vol. 2007: U.S. Census. <http://www.census.gov/population/socdemo/ancestry/Nigerian.txt > accessed April 13, 2007.

U.S. Census Bureau. 1998b. "Selected Characteristics for Persons of Ethiopian Ancestry: 1990." vol. 2007: U.S. Census. <http://www.census.gov/population/socdemo/ancestry/Ethiopian.tx t> accessed April 13, 2007.

U.S. Census Bureau. 2000. "Census 2000 Demographic Profile Highlights." vol. 2009: U.S. Census Bureau. <http://factfinder.census.gov> accessed October 15, 2009.

U.S. Census Bureau. 2007. "Percent of People 25 Years and Over Who Have Completed High School or College, by Race, Hispanic Origin and Sex: Selected Years 1940 to 2006." vol. 2007: U.S. Census.

Vickerman, Milton. 1999. *Crosscurrents: West Indian immigrants and race*. New York: Oxford University Press.

Walton, Gregory M. and Geoffrey L. Cohen. 2011. "A Brief Social-Belonging Intervention Improves Academic and Health Outcomes of Minority Students." *Science* 331:1447-1451.

Walton, Gregory M. and Geoffrey L. Cohen. 2007. "A Question of Belonging: Race, Social Fit, and Achievement." *Journal of Personality & Social Psychology* 92:82-96.

Warikoo, Natasha. 2011. *Balancing Acts: Youth Culture in the Global City*: University of California Press.

Waters, Mary C. 1999. *Black Identities: West Indian immigrant dreams and American realities*. New York: Russell Sage Foundation.

Wilkerson, Isabel. 1989. "'African-American' Favored By Many of America's Blacks." Pp. 1 in *New York Times*. New York.

Willie, Sarah Susannah. 2003. *Acting Black: College, Identity, and the Performance of Race*. New York: Routledge.

Wong, A. Carol, Jacquelynne S. Eccles, and Arnold Sameroff. 2003. "The Influence of Ethnic Discrimination and Ethnic Identification on African American Adolescents' School and Socioemotional Adjustment." *Journal of Personality* 71:1197-1232.

Zweigenhaft, Richard L. and G. William Domhoff. 1991. "Black ABC
Students in College." Pp. 68-84 in *Blacks in the White
Establishment?: A Study of Race and Class in America.* New
Haven: Yale University Press.

Index

Lightning Source UK Ltd.
Milton Keynes UK
UKOW03n1328010414

229224UK00001B/19/P